COACH,
ARE YOU CRAZY?

ANDY HAWKS

PAGE PUBLISHING, INC.
New York, NY

First originally published by Page Publishing, Inc. 2019

ISBN 978-1-64462-945-1 (Paperback)
ISBN 978-1-64462-946-8 (Digital)

Printed in the United States of America

To my grandparents, Oscar and Tacey Hawks.

CONTENTS

FOREWORD

This is a true story about an only child. A boy who grew up on a farm owned by his paternal grandparents near a small town in central North Carolina. The values he learned growing up on this farm set him on the road to remarkable success as a high school teacher and coach. His grandfather taught him many country sayings he would use throughout his life including, "If you leave this world without making it a better place than when you came into it, you have lived a wasted life."

William Anderson "Andy" Hawks has succeeded academically and athletically in football, wrestling, and track along with baseball in the public schools and at the college level of North Carolina. Andy Hawks holds degrees from Elon University in physical education and health and an undergraduate degree from Guilford College in biology. Andy participated in college at the varsity level in athletics on scholarship. During his forty-year teaching and coaching career, he has been named Coach of the Year fifteen times and to the Who's Who

Among American Teachers, three times. Andy is also a member of the North Carolina Coaching Wall of Fame. His coaching credentials include many conference and regional championships in both football and wrestling coupled with two state championships in football and several runners-up.

The den at his country home is packed with large cases full of trophies, awards, citations, and pictures of outstanding teams and athletes giving testimony to a life of incredible accomplishments.

This award-winning attitude and deeds appear as nothing unusual to this man whom we affectionately ask, "Coach, are you crazy?" His reply is always, "I'm just trying to make this world a better place for these kids we'll one day leave behind."

This roller-coaster ride in the world of athletics at the high school level, coupled with the overcoming of abnormally difficult circumstances such as death, wrecks, and a heart attack, to once again return to the sidelines, weighing the above against the endless success stories of student athletes coached by him, makes this a must-read (feel-good story): winning against all odds.

Pete Chestnut

INTRODUCTION

A mountain man and his wife, born in the early 1900s near the small Appalachian town of Galax, Virginia, would become the most influential people in my life. These were my grandparents, Oscar and Tacey Hawks. Married as teenagers, they would embark on a journey that would touch so many lives, it is hard to comprehend. These two wonderful country people made their living by farming and working in factories, mostly textile mills and the civil defense plants of World War II.

An example of their love for each other shows in the following story. My grandparents got married at a very young age, with neither one of them being sixteen years of age. As they grew older, my grandmother realized that all the young married women in the community had a wedding ring but her. Being so poor at their time of marriage, it didn't seem to be important. To quote her, "The only thing that mattered was us being together."

My grandfather was a proud owner of a beautiful blaze-faced horse with white stockings. Everyone in the community at one time or another had longed to purchase the horse from him. It being one of his most prized possessions, he didn't think of selling it. One day, while my grandmother was visiting a sister, a man came along and offered to purchase the horse from my grandfather. He sold the horse reluctantly and, immediately, found a way into town. There he purchased a beautiful wedding ring. He returned that night with the precious ring in a handsome box and gave it to her excitedly. She was so thrilled she couldn't contain herself and proceeded to make his favorite meals every night that week.

One day shortly after, she went out to visit the livestock and immediately noticed the blaze-faced horse was gone. Upon finding the horse missing, she quickly became concerned and angry. That night, as he returned from work, she was waiting on the porch for his arrival. She confronted him about the absence of the horse. He replied he had sold the horse to buy her ring. She scolded him and said, "You silly man, you sold your most prized possession." And he replied, "No, I didn't, you're my most prized possession." This love for one another allowed him to see how much she was upset about not having a wedding ring although she rarely mentioned it, but as always, the love those two had for each other found its way.

Two religious, but not overly religious people, their only indiscretion was an occasional pinch of snuff. They raised me as if I were their own, showering me with love, wisdom, and country sayings, whose applications I never even understood until my later years. My grandparents went to church when they could but not every Sunday. They lived what they learned in church and taught by example. Tacey Hawks was a wonderful homemaker, fantastic cook, and gardener. We raised most of our own food on the thirty-four-acre farm that they owned.

I took an early interest in athletics, participating in Little League football and baseball. These two mountain folk understood little about athletics, not having that much exposure as farmers growing up in an isolated rural area. However, they never missed an athletic event I participated in. One or both would always be there; win or lose, you could count on that.

Oscar and Tacey Hawks read constantly to relax and to stay informed. This home in which I grew up was always open to neighbors and friends. When I was young, in the summertime, many of my school friends would come over to play. Later they would be overwhelmed by the enormous lunch prepared by my grandmother. My little friends were in shock with the large spread of food before them, while to me, it was just normal.

My grandmother cooked three meals a day, and you had better be there and on time to eat them. When I was in high school, I'd often come home from practicing one sport or the other, and my friends would be on the porch talking to my grandmother about relationship problems or learning how to sew or crochet. Meanwhile, many of the guys learned how to drive a tractor or milk a cow or maybe even put in a fence post.

They made a house our home, and all felt welcomed. They made their home a place like you would pray your home would always be like. This wonderful support would continue right into my college years. I was lucky enough to attend what was then Elon College, allowing me to remain on the farm with the folks I loved, while having a great college experience and participating in athletics.

One of the best stories that would exemplify the love of young people, which I inherited from these loving folks would be that of my college roommate. Mike Young, from Durham, North Carolina, lived on the family farm with us during his final year of college. My grandparents and Young agreed on a rent payment due the day of our graduation.

During the year, Young ate a few meals there but worked just as though he was part of the family. On graduation day, Young, his fiancé, and myself returned to the farmhouse for Young to pay his rent before a beach trip we had planned. When Mike offered the money, my grandparents refused to take it, saying he was one of the family. My grandmother told him he had worked hard, and fair was fair.

Young asked, "Mr. and Mrs. Hawks, I can't do that."

Tacey Hawks took him to the side and said, "Mike, aren't you and that young lady going to get married?"

Young's reply was, "Yes, ma'am."

My grandmother told him to keep his money; he was going to need it for the future. "We love you and good luck." Tacey Hawks hugged my roommate, Mike, who occasionally visited them until they died. Besides raising me, their old-fashioned values and work ethic are able to live through generations. This is due to all the peoples' lives they touched, young and old, and were a part of my forty-some years of teaching on the athletic fields and in the classrooms of North Carolina.

Country counselor Oscar Hawks, until the day he died, lived with illustrious rhetoric like, "A man who doesn't respect himself certainly doesn't respect anybody else." "A man who will steal from you will lie to you as well as vice-versa." "No matter what another person does, you do what you're supposed to do, that's on you." "Always judge a person if you must judge at all by what's on the inside, not on the outside." "In God's final tally, the record will speak for the man." "Anyone can be forgiven if only they might ask." Just to name a few.

I've always considered myself that being a hard worker, for my own benefit as well as others, to be an attribute inherited from this fine man. I learned from a man who used to carry one-hundred-pound bags of cattle feed on his back on a two-mile walk from the highway where he caught a ride to work. This man also carried two screen doors on the same trek on his back home from work.

I speak very prejudiciously about a man who made his own way for himself and the love of his life, Tacey, along with their two children. A man who carried not only feed and screen doors along country roads on his back, but all of us as well, and those who were lucky enough to be touched by their wisdom, love, and teachings. I consider myself very fortunate to have been raised by these people.

CHAPTER 1

Growing Up on a Farm

Although there are many people living and working on farms throughout rural North Carolina and the United States, with agriculture being the number one industry in both, there are still stereotypes held by many. Growing up on the edge of suburbia, many of my elementary and high school classmates couldn't believe how much fun it could be to gather eggs, round up cows, chase pigs, and watch the birth of all types of animals.

I guess you could say my grandfather was my first coach. As I grew older on the farm, my responsibilities increased, and now come the experiences I would always cherish. You couldn't imagine how many country sayings you could get putting in a line of fence-post holes. Or how much you could learn about life while using a pitchfork to get up hay.

No matter what the chore, there were many things to learn from this wise coach of life on how to use your hands and your head. One summer, he got me a job in the factory where he worked while I was in high school to make extra money for the summer. Of course, I had all these great summer plans that were not to be. I asked him why he was mad at me or had I done something wrong, and he said, "If you spend a summer working in there, I believe the importance of a higher education will become clear." Guess what? He was right; I told him two things halfway through that summer job: I didn't want to do that until I was sixty-five, and I decided to go to college. Also, I explained to him half the people I worked with in the factory were good, hardworking people. The other half, I explained, were very rough around the edges, for lack of a better term. He then explained to me, "That's exactly the way it is in life too, son." So that was a very eye-opening few months.

Every summer, we spent gardening, cutting wood, putting up hay, and my grandmother canned food for the winter. Many times, while hoeing in the sun in one of the many gardens on my grandparents' farm, I'd ask the question, "Why are we raising so much when we wind up giving most of it away?" Their reply was, "You just keep hoeing." Lessons of life learned on the farm stuck with me, and I gained a respect of how much effort it took to do something and developed appreciation for things that would otherwise be lost.

Even though I have two degrees from two different universities, I many times revert to the hands-on, demanding work that has never failed me. My very first teaching check was $640 for one month's salary. When I received this first teaching check, I approached the payroll clerk for the school system to make sure of its authenticity. She informed me it was correct, and for the first time in my life, the brutal reality of how low a teacher's salary was really hit home.

I had just purchased a red four-wheel-drive 1978 F-150 pickup truck and several other items I had needed for a long time. Then this. I even asked the payroll clerk, Is the amount for two weeks or what? She replied, "That's for the month." I quickly realized I would have to supplement income with my old friend manual labor.

I quickly figured out that I would have to go back to my first coach's (my grandfather) teachings if I were to survive. I mean, I was in debt with this first big-paying job, so far that more was going out with the truck payment and other things than I had coming in. I had a decision to make. Every teacher and coach have this decision to make twice in their careers. I made the decision to coach and teach while in college and made it my passion.

I already knew the answer; I wanted to do something good with my life. Something that helped other people. Something that when my life was over, I could look back and ask, "Did my being here make any difference at all?" The answer would be, "Yes, a life that doesn't affect other lives in a positive way is a wasted life." And remember, your idea of success and your neighbors are totally different.

So with a pickup truck, two old chainsaws, and a lawn mower, Andy's Wood Service was born. Disadvantaged students and their financially disadvantaged teacher Coach Hawks began mowing grass, cutting firewood, trimming hedges, and whatever else to make it through the month. This is a program still in place today. In more than one case, I had students tell me, "I don't want to do this the rest of my life." Sounds familiar? All in all, I'm very proud of my supplementary program. It was a feature on a segment of *Fox 8 News*, "What Is Right with Our Schools?" That and the testimony of many kids for over thirty-six years make me very proud. Once again, the great coach in life, Oscar Hawks, lived on through his teachings.

We do many things in life for distinct reasons. Even the students who have helped themselves by working for me, making extra money. All had different motives that labeled success. Some were helping their parents with the bills, others were buying school clothes, while others were saving for various other things, and some were even saving for tuition for school. To this day, I have many students who call me up to reminisce and ask if I need some summer help.

I was always taught if you'll look, you can find honest work and an honest way to make money. You may not like it, but if you look hard enough, it's out there. Watching city kids work on a farm might be one of the most eye-opening and rewarding things besides teaching and coaching themselves that I have ever undertaken. Anyone who's ever taught or coached knows what I'm talking about. The look in every kid's face is unique, and it always results in a light in their eyes.

With having the privilege of growing up on a farm and now living on a farm again, I have had the opportunity to pass on to young people all the great learning experiences that I was exposed to as a child and as an adult. I know it's hard to believe, but some kids have never seen a cow unless it's on TV. This country is facing so many problems; it is neglecting one of the most obvious. Everywhere in this country, old people are passing away to leave their family farms to their children.

Farmwork being difficult and profits for farm goods being less and less bring about the sales of the family farms. Many have been in the family for generations. The land is now being sold for housing projects with sales pitches such as getting away from the hustle and bustle, moving to tranquility. A never-ending barrage of movement to the country, which eats up the old farms and ways of life.

I don't wish to step on anyone's dreams, but I have some unwelcome news. The rat race is over, and the rats have won. And with each family farm's disappearance goes our ability to grow food for this nation. Hopefully, exposure to farm life from interaction with young people will instill appreciation for the farm and its way of life. Working hard is contagious, and with each success achieved throughout comes the will to work harder next time. Being a worker is innate, being productive is innate, and we merely need something or someone to rekindle the spirits so to speak. Aha, enter the teacher/coach/tree man/farmer.

I guess by now you're saying, What's with all these references to grandpa this and grandma that? Did you have a mom and a dad? Well, yes, I did. They also lived on the farm where I grew up. My grandfather gave my mom and dad a part of the farm to build a house on shortly after I was born. My mother began working odd shifts, so my grandmother began babysitting me at an early age. A habit we never broke.

Most of my school friends that I grew up with, Gary Vincent and his sister Katie, Kenneth Roach, Tommy Rogers, Bobby Jones, etc., all have, as I do, fond memories of growing up on the farm playing the day away, eating those delicious Grandma-made lunches.

By now, you are probably wondering what happened to this beautiful farm that I have spent all this time painting a beautiful picture of. In 1983, one of my precious role models, my grandmother, was stricken with cancer and eventually died, leaving me and the love of her life on the farm alone. Things were never the same for him or me after that. We did what she asked and went on taking care of each other and living on the farm.

I worked at my profession of teaching and coaching and spent my spare time working on the farm alongside my grandfather. As the years went on, my grandfather started to fade, and in 1988, he died of natural causes. My father and his sister decided to sell the family farm much to my objection. At that moment, I went on what seemed to be a lost search to find a home much like the one I loved. I eventually found a small farm fourteen years later.

The pain of losing my grandparents and the farm is slightly softened by the fact that both of them told me at their deaths that they couldn't think anymore of me than if I were their own child. To this day, although I enjoy my present home, I still find a terrible void in my life left by the loss of my childhood homeplace. My father died of natural cases, and my mother lived on the four acres of our original homeplace my grandfather gave them. I took care of my mother until she passed away. Each time, I had to pass by my childhood homeplace on the way to see her. However, my heart is filled with sweet memories of the two people who loved all they met, working for a better world and community through arduous work and example.

Hopefully, by now, I've started to win you over. How, would you ask? By sharing the feeling that farm kids have something special. No, not squishy stuff between their toes or bib overalls, but a true understanding of what priorities in life are needed and what order they appear in your life. The things that challenging work can accomplish coupled with a can-do-never-quit attitude.

CHAPTER 2

Elementary and Junior High

This time in my life was very important to me even though I didn't realize it then. This would be a time of discovery, interaction, and my first achievement. A time of first organization and discovering what a priority was, being part of a team, and working toward a common goal. All this occurred at the same time, and ironically, I was too young and naive to even know it. But the strong men involved in all this, the great coaches I had the privilege to have teaching me, knew and exposed us to all this without us even knowing. And the best part was that they made it fun.

I went to a community elementary school, Haw River School, which included grades one to twelve. It was a giant place with three stories and a huge gymnasium and an athletic field that seemed to run on forever. This would be this short, little redheaded country boy's first real interaction with other people, especially grownups.

As you could imagine, I was scared to death. I had been kind of isolated on the farm till now.

The first day of school came. Here I would make friends, many of whom I would form lifelong bonds. After about a week of school, one day at lunch, I heard some of the guys talking about playing football. Now I knew absolutely nothing about it, but hearing the other guys my age discussing it, I had a seed planted inside of me. Haw River High School was on the third floor, Haw River Middle School was on the second floor, and Haw River Elementary School was on the first floor. We started having lunches mixed together; however, as elementary schoolers, we weren't allowed on the third floor. Most often, we'd see the high schoolers in the cafeteria when we were in there at the same time.

Here I would see my first high school football player. Integration hadn't occurred yet, so they were all white. It was the late '50s, so many had greased-back hair, white bobby socks, and penny loafers. They all had something else in common too. They were all big and wearing their varsity letter sweaters.

Here comes the dilemma: did I still want to play football? I wasn't scared by my small stature. A couple of years went by, and I bided my time, grew a little more, and concentrated on my schoolwork first. Although I was no Einstein, I worked hard. Under the tutelage of my first favorite teacher, Sybil Miller, I learned to read, write, and express myself. Ms. Miller was attractive, funny, mothering, and yes, all of us little guys had a crush on her.

I was growing some now. I still wasn't quite as big as my friends, but I discovered I could run fast enough on the farm to catch a chicken or to head off a running cow. I still didn't know how that would compare to a human, but I'd soon find out.

Football season was rolling around again, and the guys were all starting to talk, especially those who had already played a couple of years. So on the way home riding my bike, I realized I'd forgotten one obstacle to playing on the team. I'd have to talk my grandparents into it first.

Sitting at the dinner table (supper) that evening, I brought up in our usual conversations that I wanted to play football on the Little League team that met behind the school three days a week after the high school team left the field. My grandparents stopped eating and started looking at me like I had two heads.

My grandfather asked, "Where did you get an idea like that?"

I explained all my friends were playing, so I wanted to play.

Before my grandfather could say much else, my grandmother responded with a loud, "No, you're too little, and you'll get killed or broken up for life."

I was hurt, but I'd dare not say anything. Several days went by, and I had talked with my grandfather on the side, trying to get him on my side in this thing we called football. Hopefully, he could soften up my grandmother's position. Several more days went by, and I had to hurry, for practice would begin at the first of the next week. One night, after dinner, when my grandparents had retired to the living room to read, I decided to try one more time. After all, I grew up in a house where we had about five basic rules. One of those was we, as a family, could and must talk about anything. My grandmother used to say, "What affects one of us affects us all." So with all that on my mind, I brought up the subject of football one more time. Without any hesitation, my grandmother said no. Then to my surprise, my grandfather then said, "Tacey, I've been thinking, if the boy wants to play, we should let him play."

My grandmother became more resistant, saying, "He will get killed, he's too little."

My grandfather's reply was, "All his little friends are playing, and besides, he is pretty tough." Oscar Hawks explained that if they were to hold me out, and all the other kids were playing, later on, I might feel slighted.

After what seemed to be an eternal pause, my grandmother said, "Okay," then looked at my grandfather and said, "If he gets hurt, it's on you."

Excitement, anticipation, and a lot of other emotions flowed over the next several days. My grandfather took me to the sporting goods store for my first pair of football shoes. That was a Saturday to remember.

Suddenly it was Monday evening, and we had our first meeting. A lot of people showed up, almost all bigger than me. I wasn't scared, but I didn't know what to think. Then there was one man who I thought was the largest man I had ever seen. Our coach, David Ray, a gentle giant who would give me and the rest of us our first taste of football. Some of the guys had played before but not many, and even those who had played were still learning.

After coaching for over forty-some years, I now have a better appreciation of what that man had gone through. After tedious hours of showing us how to put on this hot and heavy awkward equipment, now came the running, conditioning, and teaching of the techniques like stance, blocking, and tackling. In the beginning, it was slow mo', if you know what I mean, but after many days, it was here. The day we got to hit somebody else wide open.

We got in these lines, and one by one moved up until it was our turn. So much to remember: put your mouthpiece in, keep your head up, keep your butt down, and keep your hand low to the ground, work your feet, and drive the other player out of here. And remember, don't quit till the whistle stops. Could I possibly remember all this? I hoped so. Here it comes, my time. I lined up across from one of my friends, somewhat bigger than me. Coach yelled, "Hut!" and, *bam*, we were off.

The whistle blew. I looked around but couldn't hear, for there was ringing in my ears. But I was fine. He didn't move me, and I didn't move him, but in my mind, it was a monstrous collision. I was satisfied, and everyone was yelling, "Good job, country boy!" So that was it, the recognition we all spend our lives looking for. In the years ahead, I'd receive more. Now I even call real monstrous hits and give a few as well, but that first "lick," as we call it in football, is still now rewarding and funny and a beginning of a lifelong journey in athletics. In a few practices, our numbers began to dwindle. I was sore and still trying to figure out what was going on, but I learned another valuable lesson early. Since you're still learning, many times, you may not know what to do or where to go when a play begins, but once you make up your mind, go there wide open.

After some practice time, even a novice like me soon figured out that, although I was little, I was the fastest guy on the team. This meant I got to carry the ball some, play defense, and play on the kicking team as well. This all didn't matter to me because by now, I loved the game of football.

I felt I had found my niche. A feeling I would have many times over the next forty years. We eventually won the Little League championship, even after some of our opponents had pushed older guys from upper divisions down to us.

Our gentle giant of a coach (David Ray) died in 2009. I had seen him just a few months before he passed away. The day I saw him, he was in town, sitting on a bench in front of the local tire center. He was there as I was to get some work done on his vehicle. I got out of my now-old 1978 F-150 and asked, "What are you supposed to be doing?"

He replied, "Sit down here, and let's talk about where it all went wrong."

We both were kidding, and I replied, "I'll tell you where it went wrong, when some tall guy talked me into going into coaching."

He replied, "You can't blame that on me. You did it to yourself."

We both laughed heartily and jokingly.

He then turned serious asking me about my health as I had recently had a heart attack.

I replied, "I'm fine."

He never let on the truth of how sick he truly was. I am not even sure that he knew how sick he was. A few months later, he passed away. Oh, did the community know just what it had lost? This was a man who helped so many in such a positive way. I knew what the community had lost when this fine man died.

It was time now to move on to junior high. Everything got bigger. The girls were still bigger than most of us guys. The football got bigger, and the building got bigger. By bigger, I mean, we moved. When I reached the eighth grade, we were then moved to the middle school.

Many of the local high schools like Haw River, Mebane, and others were closed to consolidate into two schools. And three local community high schools merged into one central high school. Integration was about to take place, although it had already begun as black and white students alike were enrolled at Graham Middle School. For the first time, we were on the same team with black athletes.

We learned what athleticism was. Don't get me wrong. I could still outrun my fellow teammates, but it was much harder. The transition of making new friends, teammates, and coaches began. Coach Tal Jobe, as teacher and middle-school coach from Haw River, became the Graham Middle School coach as head coach and was assisted by a former college player, Tommy Thacker, a man we all became quick to fear. His loud, gruff voice, whistle around his neck, his big frame, and chest hair protruding through a hole in his sweatshirt put us in awe. He was far from the gentle giant we had known.

In my eighth-grade year, we had PE, changed from play period. My athleticism began to develop, probably because the competition level had jumped, and I had to do my best to keep up. Classes were harder too, but we all managed to adjust. Football was tougher, my teammates and our opponents were bigger. So were the hits and speed of the game.

In the middle school, we defeated Mebane Alexander Wilson, Altamahaw Ossippie, Elon and J. H. Cobb of Yanceyville. This set up a showdown with undefeated E. M. Holt, and you can guess, the Graham Middle School Satans. We played on a cold Saturday night. Even some of our kinfolk from out of town came to watch.

On defense now, I had been moved to defensive end. By now, I had become a hitter, and from our scouting reports, they (E. M. Holt) had a one-man show in running back Daryl Green, who was twice our size and very fast. For the first time playing football, I would encounter an opponent who, when I hit him, it may have hurt me more than it did him.

However, I tackled him every time he came near me and sometimes away from me. The hitting was the hardest of the season. We dropped three touchdown passes in the end zone. That would later spell our doom. They scored first, and then we scored, making every possession crucial. In the end, when the horn blew, we had lost. Our first taste of defeat in a game that really mattered. In the locker room, while turning in our equipment, everyone including the coaches were crying and yes, me too.

Hard to understand losing when you've been taught all your life to do the very best you can do, and you'll succeed. What to do when you've done the first part and don't succeed? My grandfather later explained, "Sometimes, less times than not, you fail for a reason. Sometimes you don't succeed now, so you can succeed later and appreciate it more." No matter what, it still hurt. I felt like I had been run over by a bus.

To quote a high school coach I'd have later, Coach Don Amos, "Everything hurts when you lose, Andy." Was he ever right. Despite the terrible loss, the thrill of all those other victories, coupled with the many new friendships we cultivated that year was a success. Remember that big assistant coach, Coach Tommy Thacker? You know, the one with the body hair sticking out the hole of his sweatshirt? I think on the night of that loss, he cried more than all of us. That big gruff man was just like us after all.

Boyd Pearson, the quarterback on the middle school football team, would also be a high school teammate, along with many others on that team. Later, he and I would coach together at our good ol' alma mater, Graham High School.

CHAPTER 3

High School

By now, I guess you've noticed sometimes I refer to myself as "country boy," a term I feel is beloved. Some others had used it toward me in a not-so-flattering way, but that's their problem. By now, this country boy has spoken of how fast things moved from elementary to junior high school, especially in athletics. Now we're ready for a real jump.

Many of my high school football teammates would sign scholarships with UNC at Chapel Hill, NC State, Duke, A&T, and so forth. I realized even then I was in very special company. High school started in the late '60s for me. Before classes started we had "football camp," which began with a team meeting on a Sunday afternoon and continued with three practices a day all week long, eating and sleeping on the campus.

About Wednesday, you were asking yourself if you really wanted to keep doing this, even though you knew the answer. Sleepless nights didn't help any because we all had to sleep in the gym. Hot, sore, and tired were synonymous with football camp. Everyone was waiting for Saturday, tired of prankster teammates who might put foot powder in your hair in the dark or pour aftershave on your genitals while you slept. Oh, and the freshmen guys, which I was now a part of, caught the worst of it from the upper classmen. It was a kind of an initiation, if you will.

By now, we were beginning to adjust to our three new coaches. I would meet a man who would influence my life even today. Then head coach Bill Joye, defensive and line coach Don Amos, and Coach Harold Smith. Coach Smith would later become the wrestling coach. But that's another story.

Coach Bill Joye challenged you every day in every practice. He spoke in a stern voice but was always supportive, knowledgeable, highly organized, and always there. Coach Don Amos, a mountain man who had played college football and tempered everything with a country/ mountain man–type of humor, occasionally screamed and yelled, but eventually ended it with a smile. Coach Harold Smith came from a family of means, was knowledgeable, and had a real quality you really admired. He cared.

So here we go with three outstanding coaches, a bevy of talent, and a very supportive student body. Sounds like all you need, right? Integration had hit, closing the local black school, and moving the white students over to Central High, which was originally an all-black school. Now it would be called Graham High School.

Of course, much animosity would be held by the black population, and rightly so. However, we as students felt almost helpless to do anything about the situation or knew what to do. The first day of practice found us all introducing ourselves to one another, and all seemed to go well until someone made a racial comment at waterbreak. After that, all hell broke loose. Once everything had settled down, we went back to practice, and the integration thing would not affect us as a team again, or so we thought.

After a Friday night football game with Southern Durham, a riot broke out in the parking lot, which went on for four hours. Many left, but many stayed. I left after the game and explained to my grandfather what had happened when I got home. Being told I must treat everybody the same as I would want to be treated, I just assumed that everybody felt the same way. But then he explained things that had happened to the blacks over the years that would be hard to easily forget, and that you couldn't understand unless they happened to you. Not till much later would I more fully understand. With the school closed and the entire town under curfew, we later learned that many of the same things were happening throughout the entire country.

As the school year resumed, racial tensions still existed, but many chose, especially me, to ignore and go on. After all, I had no hard feelings toward anybody. Football ended that season with a better than five-hundred record, and we were beginning to build.

By now, it's November, and we had already experienced changing classes at the middle school, so that wasn't a problem. The classes were in different buildings so that meant we could see more friends at class change. Coach Bill Joye asked me, or should I say strongly suggested to me, that I wrestle as soon as football was over. So being hooked on the athletic program as I was, how could I refuse? After all, who could whip the strong country boy, right? I went out for wrestling and discovered I was one of only four freshmen on the team. This was great until I learned everybody else was seniors. We would go on to have a wonderful team record, but we four freshmen were going to get killed every day at practice.

We were the ones they showed or practiced the moves or maneuvers on. Often, there was more than one person in our weight class, so we'd have challenge matches to see who would get to wrestle. Only one person could represent the school at a time. I personally fit into the one-hundred-thirty-pound category or weight class. We were so lucky to have a defending state champion on our team, Wayne Riggings. He personally took me under his wing. He was a senior, a champion, and he knew how to win. He sometimes stayed late to help me work on moves. Before you knew it, I had won a challenge match and was in the starting lineup.

I was starting in a varsity wrestling match. And as soon as it began, I suddenly forgot everything I had been taught, fear took over, and I relied mostly on my country boy's strength. After all, everybody else had been in the weight room while I had been lifting bales of hay. I managed to get a takedown, shoot a nifty cradle, a maneuver I learned, and pinned my opponent. I had pinned a senior and won the first match I had ever wrestled. I went on to win my next three matches in a row. Three wins and no defeats. Once again, I had found my niche, or so I had thought.

I proceeded to lose the next sixteen straight matches. So much for freshman success. I made up my mind that summer I was either not ever going to wrestle again or get very good at what I was doing. I saved up some money from working on the farm, and I sent myself to the wrestling camp at Appalachian State University that summer. It was harder than anything I had ever done to that point. Three hard sessions of wrestling at night, films, and at the end of camp, a tournament. I was asked if I could stay on an extra week to get in some time with the college wrestlers. Great idea for the long run, however, a bad immediate idea.

After all, up to now, the sweat-and-tears road is about all I knew. I got better though, and by my next season up, I had a winning record. I was the captain of the team. Unwelcome news though, all the seniors graduated, leaving me and one other sophomore the only people who had ever wrestled before on the team. One of four football coaches, Harold Smith, was appointed to coach wrestling. He admittedly had never seen any wrestling before this, so I would sit beside him during matches and help show moves or maneuvers during practice. My coaching career had begun, and I didn't even know it.

To his credit, Harold Smith constantly read books, magazines, and attended seminars on wrestling. Four years later, he would leave our school and go on to win a state team championship at Trinity High School. In the meantime, we needed help now. Contrary to our woes, we had a winning season as a team. My wrestling success continued with winning many conference and regional championships.

My football and wrestling skills continued to develop all to my unawareness. It was gradual, in the meantime, so to speak. I needed more money than I was making farming, so one of my classmates, Judy Phillips (I called her Ann), told me she had gotten a job at Wrike Drug Company in downtown Graham, right down the street from the courthouse (the big time). There I went to work for Larry McAllister, the proprietor and head pharmacist, and fellow pharmacist Dale Thompson. I would develop a friendship that would help mold many outlooks on my life, values that would also stay with me throughout my life.

Many special characters worked at Wrike Drug during the 1970s. Besides the two distinguished gentlemen I mentioned earlier, there were my good friend Ann Phillips and Handy Senior. Handy was a fix-it-all maintenance man, who did everything from deliver door-to-door to grinding ice. That's right, we had ice delivered, then shaved it with a machine and placed it in the front of the soda fountain.

The two proprietors were University of North Carolina fans. Don't ask me why. A guy who used to have my job was a Graham native, named Greg Miles. He worked the counter, serving drinks, chips, hot sandwiches, and delivered prescriptions, just as I did now. Greg knew the players at UNC—Phil Ford, Rick Fox, and many other Carolina basketball players, who visited the little drugstore I regularly worked in during high school.

Later, I discovered that Larry McAllister, the owner of Wrike Drug and my boss, and his sidekick pharmacist Dale Thompson, were graduates of the Carolina Pharmacy School, so that explains the association with

Greg Miles. He was a basketball manager during the Dean Smith era at Carolina, which illuminates the visitation of UNC royalty.

I always worked the night shift after school, after whatever practice was in season and every other Saturday. One day after work, Ann Phillips, Patty Pierce, a coworker, and myself started working on a plan to play hooky from school one day in the upcoming week. So after much deliberation, we decided that Ann or Judy, myself, and Patty with her boyfriend would take a day off and go to Tanglewood Forest Park in Winston-Salem, North Carolina, a ride about one hour from my house.

We had the perfect plan: we'd all meet in the high school parking lot on Thursday morning after homeroom. The girls packed this delicious picnic basket, and we put it in the trunk of my classic 1969 Mustang Fastback for an adventure at Tanglewood Park. The day arrived, and we all skipped the day at school. A new member, Janet Harrison, decided she'd go too along with a fellow classmate we'll call Dean. We jumped into my car in the Graham High School parking lot and headed to Tanglewood Park.

Upon arrival, we all changed into our bathing suits and proceeded to ride the rides, row the canoes, and feed the ducks. We all went swimming and enjoyed the delectable picnic basket the girls had prepared. Eventually, the day slipped away, and by then, we all felt that we had no responsibility, just having a lot of fun. We were swum out, ate all the chicken in the picnic basket, and realized it was time to head home.

We packed up the Mustang and headed back. With perfect timing, we arrived at the school just as it was letting out. I pulled into the parking lot; the girls and guys got into their respective cars and went home. Call me dumb. I went down to the field house to football practice with not a word from anyone.

It was two weeks later, and all seemed well. We had all returned to school the next day after our Tanglewood getaway, time had passed uneventfully, and pretty much, my fellow skippers and I had almost forgotten about our trip. It was business as usual; nobody asked for a note to return to class the next day. Everything was pretty normal around the farm. Then one morning, while eating breakfast, my grandfather asked, "How did you enjoy your vacation last week?"

With a mouthful of cornflakes, I asked, "What vacation?"

He replied, "The one you and Ann Phillips took to Tanglewood a couple of weeks ago."

I responded, "How did you find out about that?"

And he said, "Never you mind, I can't reveal my sources."

After many moments of silence, I inquired, "You're not mad?"

"No."

"Promise you are not going to get mad about it?" I, of course, questioned, to which he said, "What do I have to be mad about? You are going to be grounded for six weeks, and I know how long it takes to get from that high school on the hill to our home. You come home every day right after football practice. No TV, no telephone, no coming or going."

I then asked him, "What are you so upset about? Nobody got hurt, and everything went smooth."

He said, "You're right, but something could have happened, a wreck, not even your fault, that could have ended your life or even your friends' lives, when you were supposed to be in school. But all of us, especially those other kids' families, would have had to pay a terrible price. You skipped school, and you are right, nothing bad happened, but it could have. Son, when you don't do the right thing, anything can happen. So you're grounded because you were supposed to be in school."

The next six weeks would be some of the longest of my life. During the next weeks, I wasn't allowed to speak to anyone off our farm. I remember one Saturday I had to rake the yard, and some of my friends drove up in a 1969 Chevelle. I began a conversation when my grandfather came out of the house and calmly walked up to the car, took the rake out of my hand, took me by the arm, and told my friends, "He's on lockdown. Come back in six weeks, and y'all can visit all you want."

Everybody laughed with me being the butt of the joke as my grandfather continued leading me away to the opposite part of the yard. My friends quickly left, not mad, but laughing. My grandfather pointed out a spot in the yard I had missed and went into the house. This strong man who had raised me once again had taught me a meaningful lesson without raising a hand. There are consequences in life, good and bad, to whatever you do.

My high school time was full of ups and downs, just like life is today. During my junior year in high school, we went to play Southern Alamance, a cross-county rival. Many of us had played on the same Little League teams earlier in life. This was a big game, working for a play-off spot. The team who won would get into the state playoffs, and the other team would go home. Football always seemed to make for a lot of emotions. After all, many of Southern's team had played with and against us in Little League. However, we won both games my junior and senior years. We garnished the bragging rights for Graham since both schools had a Graham address.

On the other hand, as a wrestling team, we barely broke even, but I enjoyed some success winning many tournaments and conference championships. In my junior and senior years of school, I was all-conference, all-state, and so on and so on, quickly developing without noticing it.

Suddenly it was almost time for graduation. I had hoped to go to college and, after careful thought, arrived at a major. I decided to go into teaching. I wanted to do something with my life that would hopefully affect the world long after I was gone. I wanted to do for others what so many wonderful people had done for me, such as Coach Ray, Coach Bill Joye, Coach Tommy Thacker, and my grandfather.

In June of 1973, I graduated from high school, humbly winning seven awards. I had been awarded an athletic scholarship to Elon College to wrestle. I was very excited and scared at the same time to attend Elon. I had wrestled in the summer of my high school year, winning the United States Freestyle Championship, so I felt somewhat prepared. For all that, I felt myself an average student, and I knew it would take my best effort. Here I would meet some of the best athletes I had ever faced. People who could run as fast or faster than me, and the wrestling was brutal. The toughest match I ever had in high school was like that every day in college practice.

In the city, county, and conference wrestling tournaments during my senior year in high school, I was approached by a man who would not only become one of my coaches in college but a great friend, Coach Mickey Brown. He contacted me after a win in the semifinal matches in the conference wrestling tournament. He was a giant of a man from Asheboro, North Carolina, and a former defensive end at East Carolina University. He introduced himself and told me he wanted me to come to Elon, on a wrestling scholarship. How ironic was that, I mean, we were standing at the time in the Elon Alumni Gym.

CHAPTER 4

College Years

I was proud and excited. I couldn't wait to get home and tell my grandparents. Little could I know the great challenge before me. I graduated in June, leaving my alma mater, Graham High School, behind, but not forever.

The adjustments at Elon were difficult, but no more challenging than they seemed to my peers. For the first time we were in college together, with all the other students in the county, some of whom we had played against in high school; also, students from the northern United States and from other countries. I hadn't realized how much this mixing of cultures could make you see things on such a broader scale.

The professors we had were excellent. I was a PE major, and at the time, there were so many of us, it seemed it would be impossible to find a job upon graduation. Consequently, I decided to double major in biology. After all, PE, athletics, and science had always been my strong suits in high school. I was interested, committed, and energetic, and raring to go.

Biology classes were interesting but very hard, and in the labs, sometimes, I didn't know what they were talking about, but we all soon settled in for a learning adventure. In the literature department, we had Dr. Owens and Dr. Priestly, the latter being of English origin. She spoke with a heavy accent that held your attention. One time in class while handing back a batch of freshly graded papers, she inquired, "Hawks, what is your major?" I quickly answered, "Teaching. I am going to be a teacher, and someday, hopefully, a coach."

She then replied, "Don't turn your back on your writing. You write very well."

I never gave it much thought until now. So, well, we'll let you be the judge.

PE classes were great since back when I had a lot of energy I enjoyed playing a sport, and for the first time, I was playing sports that I had little experience with like soccer, handball, tennis, and table tennis. In fundamentals of PE class, I met Janie Brown, the wife of Coach Mickey Brown, a professor who remains a beacon for many of us even today. She went out of her way to teach us that every kid needed special attention, and that students remember their teachers their entire lives. So make sure you do your best because you're always being watched; a role model you'll always be, so be a good one. Mickey Brown, Janie's husband, on the other hand, would always make us laugh with one of his stories, which you could always apply to your situation. An example was one time while he was teaching driver's education in Fayetteville, North Carolina. A student who had been struggling finally seized an opportunity to drive. With three other students in the car, she drove on to a four-lane road, and as she seemed to be responsive to any instructions, Coach Brown told her to give it a little more gas because everyone was passing them. Without hesitation, she stomped on the gas and sped up very quickly. Suddenly, Coach Brown said, "Hey, hey, slow down a little," so she stomped on the brake. The driver's education car immediately spun around and wound up in the opposite direction, and the engine cut off while we were facing four lanes of oncoming traffic."

Coach Brown said, "Hey, Hawks, I felt like getting out and running myself, but I stayed with it. Hey, Hawks, sometimes in life, you gotta just stay with it."

I asked him how the story ended. He said, "They finally got the car cranked." He switched driving responsibilities with the other students, they got the car turned around and headed in the right direction.

Dr. Allen White, the athletic director at Elon and an inspiring classroom teacher, was very professional. He taught us that when coaching your players, no matter the sport, they will act (especially in high school) just like you do. They emulate good or bad behavior, and sometimes both. Dr. Allen White, Janie Brown, and Coach Mickey Brown exemplified professionalism and made sure you understood the meaning of the word. Some of the greatest coaches were regular folks teaching classes at Elon. Coach Kay Yow, a nationally recognized women's basketball coach and who succumbed to cancer and was the women's US Olympic basketball team, was an instructor of mine at Elon as well as the Elon women's basketball coach.

I had some of the greatest coaching minds in the country helping me get started. Later, it would pay off in dividends. The respect of those folks, many of whom would go on to become not only mentors but friends, would prove invaluable. All these outstanding people taught me to work at my craft and learn from others who had been successful. They instilled in me that so many young coaches thought coming out of school they had it all figured out, when, although being very talented, they had only begun to scrape the surface. The abovementioned coaches had taught me and my fellow classmates that coaching is a continual lifelong learning process. When you quit learning, you become stagnant, and then you become complacent, and that's not fair to the kids you teach and coach.

Many of those friendships that were established during my four years at Elon, from 1973 to 1977, would be irreplaceable in my life. By now, the wisdom of all the coaching legends I interacted with seemed to have laid my foundation for success. But no one would know the obstacles in the future I was going to face. They say for each tragic event you live through, it takes a piece of you with it. I certainly believe that, for in the years ahead, tragedy and success, loss and victory, character tests, the loss of idols would all play a part in my coaching growth and transformation.

My wrestling career at Elon flourished under the tutelage of Coach Mickey Brown. However, football, one of my biggest loves, had slowed to a crawl due to three severe knee surgeries during the summer between my freshman and sophomore years in college. They were all cartilage issues. I had played most of my senior year in high school with cartilage damage and great pain. My grandfather met with the doctor who had done my first knee surgery, and the doctor had told him, "I don't see how your young man stood the pain. He had a piece of cartilage partially torn from the bone still connected to the joint and actually stuck in the hinge at the same time." When asked by the doctor, "How long has he been playing football and wrestling on that knee?" my grandfather responded, "Several years." The doctor said, "Fascinating. He must have been in so much pain." That seemed to be the story of my life. I could always stand physical pain, but emotional pain like losing my family farm, my grandparents' and many mentors' deaths seemed to stick with me forever.

Despite my knee problems, my wrestling career at Elon flourished. I learned a lot of self-discipline. I had a lot of interaction with some outstanding people, learned a lot of wrestling techniques, and prepared myself for many victories and, yes, unfortunately, many disappointments. No, not the disappointments on the wrestling mat, but political disappointment. You see, until graduation from Elon, this educated country boy hadn't even known about politics, especially in education.

After all, we were going to be teaching for the kids, or so I thought. I spent many days running the streets of Greenway Park, a housing development near the farm I grew up on in high school and college, trying to cut weight for the upcoming matches. Dieting and running had been a part of my life and would continue for the next four years.

In 1977, I graduated from Elon with two conference championships in wrestling and a high national ranking to go out and face the world. After much job searching in the PE area, I realized I was just two courses short of having my biology degree from Elon. So rather than going back for an entire year, I attended Guilford College just up the highway from Elon in Greensboro, North Carolina. It only required me to take two final biology classes to receive my biology degree.

CHAPTER 5

Career

Armed with the ability to teach and coach and out of athletic eligibility, I graduated from Guildford College in 1979 with a biology degree, having paid for it with my farming money. After one year of performing my job as the offensive coordinator in Martinsville, Virginia, I wound up at Bartlett Yancey High School in Caswell County, North Carolina. Here I would start one of my long stints in coaching. It kinda fit at the time. I mean, Caswell County was a very rural place, and I was a country boy so, hey, as Coach Brown would say, a perfect fit.

I lived on the farm with my grandparents and drove back and forth to Yanceyville, the location of the school, just as I had to Martinsville, Virginia, right up Highway 87 N. I was the offensive coordinator, just as I was in Martinsville. We played for the state championship there and lost, so hey, here we go again.

A new job after only a year. I was the PE teacher, biology teacher, football coach, wrestling coach, and basketball coach as well. Oh, it gets better. At one point, I was teaching math, biology, physical science, health and physical education while coaching football, wrestling, basketball, and baseball.

Superman, you say? At the time, I didn't think so. You're young and dumb. But as time went on, I realized how full my plate was. I was also in charge of the Monogram club. This was the club who holds session on all those athletes who will receive varsity letters.

Now, I know you are saying, "Coach, are you crazy?" This is a question you'll ask yourself over and over as you continue to read this book, hence the name. After eight years in Caswell County, we became very proud of our accomplishments. Although we didn't do well in football, our wrestling and baseball flourished. My conference championships and tournament championships followed. Now, keep in mind I was driving thirty-some miles one way to work. I was holding down all these teaching and coaching positions at the same time, and the conference participation had many times required me to drive right by my house on the way to a match or a game. Then upon its completion, go right back by my house (the farm I grew up on back to Yanceyville). Then get in the Mule and come home. Oh, what's the Mule, you ask? That's the nickname the kids I coached gave the old 1978 Ford pickup. If anyone could even see just the number of kids that thing has hauled home in its lifetime, it would probably look like a remake of the singing of "We Are the World." The Mule was bought at County Ford in Graham in 1978. Brand new. It now has over 900,000 miles on the original motor. It also doubles as a workhorse in our farm and tree company. She doesn't look like she used to, but I remember that beautiful candy-apple red paint and my grandparents standing beside it. That truck I still drive every day has hauled kids home, firewood, people to the hospital, on and on, for many years. In my last job at Hugh M. Cummings High School, we had about six to eight kids every day I hauled home who didn't have a ride. I would reach a point and let them all off at the same spot. They would all go in different directions. "See ya later, Coach." Tomorrow it would be the same thing all over again. We'll talk more about the Mule later.

Let's talk about the remarkable friends I made at Bartlett Yancey, my second job. Athletic director Lindsey Page, who holds a place close to me in the NC Coaching Wall of Fame. Gaye Poteat, a beautiful tall lady who graduated from Bartlett Yancey and returned after graduation to become a chief cog in the working of the school, as lead secretary and cheerleading advisor. This admirable person has dedicated her life to the school and community in which she grew up and loves. She still serves today in that very same capacity.

Even though I loved the people and kids of Caswell County, I still had that urge to return home. To be specific, I wanted to return to Graham High School to coach a team in which I felt I had a lot of unfinished business. Championships to be won, kids to be coached, and putting something back where I grew up. I enjoyed my time in Caswell County, and we won four conference championships in wrestling. I coached some football players who went on to be outstanding players.

One time, my ninety-eight-pounder conference champion, an unassuming senior, asked me while I was working at Bartlett Yancey if I would go to court with him as a character witness. I responded, "What did you do?" He said he got caught with his girlfriend in the back seat of her mama's car on a late Sunday night. The Caswell County sheriff's department had caught one of my star wrestlers. So as far as I knew, he was a senior, isolated country boy, kind of small, unassuming, and quiet. The day for his trial arrived, so we headed up the street to the courthouse. On the way up there, with both of us in suits and ties, I asked him, "This might be simple. Have you ever been in trouble with the law before?"

This small fellow said, "Yes, I killed a man."

I slammed on the brakes in the truck and said, "What!"

He continued, "One night, my father came home drunk and started beating on my mother. I shouted for him to stop, but of course, he didn't. So I asked him again, expecting the same nonresponse. He was hurting her really bad, and it was not the first time. I couldn't bear it anymore, so I grabbed a shotgun from behind the wall, and I killed him. I was exonerated in court, so here I am."

Of course, if you're like me, you were in shock. But we continued our journey up to the courthouse, me not knowing what my testimony would do. On the one hand, I had a student athlete who had done nothing but what I had asked of him, and yet a part of me was still reeling. How do you testify to someone's fine character when you know this other information? Oh, don't get me wrong. I knew his feelings. So I just went on to the courthouse and testified to what I knew about him, this student athlete I had known since he was a freshman.

Another remarkable athlete who was a star at Bartlett Yancey was a three-sport athlete; he was all conference in football and wrestling and track, plus throwing the shot put. This young man we'll call Michael was an inspiration to all of us.

He had many athletic scholarships, and with great grades, it would seem elementary to accept one, right? Well, I thought so. My alma mater, Elon College, wanted him to play football and wrestle. Elon College, now

University, wanted him. So everything seemed to be okay, right?

This fine athlete came to me one day after talking it over with his father, looking very depressed and informed me that he couldn't go to Elon because they had sent some financial aid papers to their home, and his father had become enraged and refused to fill them out. There were questions like how much their home was worth and other financial information. This smart young man was distraught. He thought his father was beyond any con-versation, so he said, "Coach, I don't know what to do."

So I told him, "It'll be okay, I'll go and talk to him."

Michael told me it would never work. "Coach, he's a very stubborn man. He's got the idea in his head that we are all going to work and live on that farm the rest of our lives."

So suddenly, I'm faced with a kid who is really feeling lost. The moon is his goal, and he's going to be relegated to hoeing potatoes. Of course, knowing me by now, you know I couldn't let this opportunity go by, especially for this exceptional young person, high school captain of the football team, the captain of the wrestling team, and valedictorian of his class.

I drove my young athlete home one day, especially to talk with his father about this young man's future. This burly middle-aged black man was hoeing tobacco in the middle of a large field, a task I hadn't been unfamiliar with. I introduced myself to this huge man, built with a large framework like his son. I began to explain what wonderful opportunities were awaiting his son. A scholarship to Elon College, the coaches there having offered him a full ride in football, and they wanted him to wrestle too. But his biggest drawback, the only drawback, was his father not allowing him to leave the farm. This noble, loving father told me to my face, even after I had approached him in the middle of the tobacco field, that his son didn't need to go to college. He told me he appreciated it, even after my long spiel, but his son didn't need to go to college. He was going to spend the rest of his life working on the family farm. Then the irony hit. Here I was, now educated, wanting to spend the rest of my life on the family farm, and here was a man wanting things the old way: for all his children to grow up and live on the family farm.

Later on, I approached that man in the field again right before graduation. He told me after my pleading about his son's wasting talents and needs that if he ever saw me again, he would probably do me harm, and he wasn't lying. What happened to Michael? He joined the armed services. He became a colonel, an all-state wrestler, and all-world football player. He may not have wound up where he thought he would, but he was a winner, and winners never lose out. My grandfather, Coach Mickey Brown, and Coach Bill Joye had taught me years ago that you can't run out on life, or it will run out on you. Michael Jones came to visit me. Oh, we've just been calling him Michael. He is now an army colonel living in Colorado. He has contacted me frequently even though we haven't seen each other in many years.

He went to the farm where I grew up looking for me many times, only to be told to find me somewhere else. His most meaningful message was, "I have four children of my own. Until I became a father, I didn't realize how much you did for us. I just wanted to tell you thank you. I'd understood you had been in some bad health lately, and before something happens to either one of us, I wanted to tell you thank you." I asked him what had happened for him to suddenly realize this. He said he had a farm of his own; he was a big contractor in Colorado. How he wound up there, who knows? But it touched me as he told me he worried something would happen with either one of us before he got to tell me how much he appreciated what I had done for him while I was coaching him during the 1970s. He said, "I know what you went through now, and you did a lot more for us than you were required to. For that, Coach, I want to thank you." He continued, "Coach, I'll never be able to repay what you have done for me."

I immediately gave him my full patented answer. "Someday, son, you'll run upon a young man who is going to need a little more help than others to find himself. That's when you step in, and those that have been picked on, you pick them up, give the same helping hand I gave you, and it will be okay."

During my thirty-five-mile commute, I put many miles on my faithful old 1987 Ford F-150 pickup truck. After all, sometimes it went from Graham to Yanceyville seven days a week. Not just for school, but Saturday all day, wrestling tournaments, and Sunday football coaches' meetings. Believe it or not, that old truck is still doing duty. After eight years of running up and down the highway every day, not to mention my home responsibilities, I began to get very weary.

CHAPTER 6

Everything Changes

In 1982, something unimaginable happened. My inspiration, my beloved grandmother, came in to my room one morning and asked me if I could go with her to the doctor that day if she was able to get an appointment. In haste, I twirled around and asked her what the matter was. She said she had a knot on her side, and she wanted to check about it. She made an appointment for several days later. We went to the UNC Medical Center in Chapel Hill, North Carolina, for extensive testing. The doctor was not immediately sure what the problem was. But on the way home, she informed me the area in question had suddenly become very sore. Surgery was scheduled to find out more answers. When the doctor returned, he informed our entire family that our precious grandmother and my surrogate mother had cancer. They had removed as much of it as possible, but further treatments would be needed. That same year, with all her family at her bedside, she died. The farm and my grandfather would never be the same again. Nor would any of us. People talk about strength and character, but until they watch a wonderful, strong, remarkable person like her fight this dreaded disease, they just don't understand. One night, sick and weakened from the horrible chemotherapy treatments, she rose from her bed and summoned me to the kitchen. There she began to get out pots and pans, and I asked, "Grandma, what are you doing? You need to be in the bed." She told me to be quiet and pay attention. "I'm going to give you a crash cooking lesson. When something happens to me, you and your grandfather will starve to death." I didn't have the heart to tell her that I could barely boil water. I watched for a while then finally convinced her to go to bed. Could anyone believe this woman was actually on her deathbed, and here she was worried about everyone else?

How much she had suffered, no one could ever imagine. She never said a word. I finally understood the meaning of courage. My grandfather and I continued to live on the farm until his death six years later.

During my coaching and teaching at Bartlett Yancey, I met a lady who worked in the office. She and her husband befriended me and my grandfather, sending me home with homemade meals. Between Libba and my aunt's cooking and my mother cooking next door, we made out pretty good. My grandfather became a pretty good cook himself; however, I guess there is no hope for me. I can still barely boil water.

My longing to return to Alamance County grew stronger, especially to my strong roots in Graham. With my grandfather now there by himself on the farm, I felt that I needed to be working closer to home.

One day, at a home track meet in Yanceyville, our opponent was my alma mater, good ol' Graham High. I already knew most of the athletes; after all, they were neighborhood kids. I introduced myself to Graham's head track coach, who also served as the head football coach. I made a lifelong friend, Jim Mach. A tall Texan and former Wake Forest football player, we would begin a journey the next year that would be tremendous fun and of help to many future generations.

I would return to Yanceyville many times, sometimes to play football, sometimes to wrestle, and sometimes to visit with friends. The last time, however, was as I made many short weekly visits spending time with the Walkers until my friend Libba died with the dreaded cancer in 2008. Another valiant fight lost and a great amount of suffering going on without letting the rest of us know how really bad it was.

So now it's around 1985, and I am home. I'm back teaching and coaching at my alma mater. Funny how big that place looked in my senior year. Now the halls looked tiny, minute even. Funny that half of the teachers that taught me were still there. The rest retired, some had died, and some had just changed jobs. Coach Don Amos didn't coach football anymore, but he did coach girls' basketball. My new friend, Coach Jim Mach, was there. And an old-time coaching rival-now-teammate, Coach Chuck Maynard, now deceased. He was a fine friend and coach. The kids called him the Bear because of his burly appearance and giant paws for hands. A gruff person who was really a softie, the kids loved him because of his knowledge of the game and his sincerity for their success.

I found out a long time ago from some pretty special people like Dr. Janie Brown, Lindsey Page, and others soon to follow that you can't fool the kids. You give off a vibe that exudes enthusiasm, knowledge, and an inexhaustible work ethic and a sincerity of whether you really are about their success, or if you are just out there for yourself or your own prestige. The kids can tell, believe me. He or she may not be able to remember a scientific theory or an algebraic equation, but they can tell if your heart is in what you are doing.

They'll work just as hard as you do. Once, while I was at Graham, we had a car wash for the wrestling team to raise money for new uniforms. Well, Mr. Organization assigned the kids shifts on which they were to work. I talked a local bank into letting us use their parking lot and water, so everything was ready, right? The bank was in downtown Graham, so they were glad to help out. At eight o'clock on Saturday morning, here we go. So roll up your sleeves, right? I had it all planned out. I'd supervise the kids, and they would show up in shifts; I'd collect the money and sit in the shade.

Wrong. As long as I would work, the kids would work. As soon as I sat down, they would sit down. By the end of the day, I had worked all three shifts, washed about eighty cars, and I was red as a lobster. We made all the money needed for our uniforms, but I slept the entire Sunday following that event.

Another lifetime friend would become part of my return to my alma mater. Luther Turner, a tall athletic coach, who was a local high school football star, and later became the same coach at Johnson C. Smith University in Charlotte, North Carolina.

We all had different coaching styles and sometimes different theories on how and what was to be done. But we all agreed on one thing: keep whatever you do or say positive. It's okay to tell a kid he's wrong or doing something wrong. Just make sure you go back shortly thereafter, put your arm around his neck, and say something positive.

After all, even with his love for what we're trying to get done, this same kid who couldn't remember the scientific theory or an algebraic equation can soon figure out there are other places he can be successful. Not all of them good, so stay positive.

All of us tried to serve as role models, all in diverse ways. The Bear (Coach Maynard) and Jim Mach served as the heads of different clubs. Luther was in charge of the intramural programs. He really had it going on at lunch. A lot of the kids had signed up to play basketball, Wiffle ball, and other games. What is Wiffle ball? It's just like softball but indoors, with a hollow plastic bat and a plastic ball with holes in it. Once I moseyed over to the gym at lunch to watch an intramural Wiffle ball championship game. Coach Luther Turner was behind the plate umpiring the game; a rather heavy young girl hit the ball hard and slung the bat, striking Coach Turner on her way to first base. Coach Turner shouted, "You're out!" The girl returned to pick up the bat, fussing for what she considered to be a bad call. Coach Turner then explained, "You slung the bat and hit me too, you know you are out." The girl walked away laughing.

Me, I kept up my usual on-the-job training. I hired kids, especially the less fortunate ones, to mow grass, cut firewood, and work on the farm on the weekends and in the summers. We all put up hay, worked with cows, and other farm chores. You won't believe this: one of my ex-athletes from those 1985 adventures still works for me today, as well as his son. I guess we're still affecting future generations.

Teaching at Graham High was kinda neat. Many of the students in class were neighbor kids or kids of people I had gone to school with. One time, while handing out football equipment, I found a pair of shoulder pads with my name on the inside of them. Boy, that brought back memories. To add to the uniqueness of seeming to go back in time, our starting quarterback was the son of my former high school coach, Bill Joye. David Joye, at over six feet tall, and a gifted athlete, was a team captain and leader who'd later become a player for Clemson University.

Graham High wasn't the same school I'd graduated from. Oh yeah, the buildings were the same. The kids had many of the same names I'd gone to school with. The zone that Graham High had to pull students from had shrunk so adversely, the school's population had decreased, which made the student body much smaller than all the other schools. We were now playing in a 3-A classification with a high 2-A enrolled student body.

Wrestling, basketball, and smaller-numbered sports don't seem to have been affected as much. But football, where mass numbers to participate are needed to prevent fatigue and injury, now that's a different problem.

We felt like we'd have to be in better condition, better coached, and better organized to compete with larger schools. We were right. With David Joye, Tony Pinnix, Lonnie Thompson, and some other standout coaches, we had a chance. Bill Joye told me two things about coaching football that really stuck. First, get your average players better than your adversaries by coaching and conditioning. The talented players are always going to be talented. It's when you get your average players better than theirs, that's when you win football games. Also, his familiar phrase, "Blocking and tackling, Coach. All these fancy formations are worthless if they can't block and tackle."

To this day, when watching football films, looking for tendencies, strengths, and weaknesses, those words of my high school coach echo within me. After all, I wound up calling the offensive plays at Graham with my old high school coach's son, pulling the trigger and making things happen. I felt a lot of self-pressure. But even with my old mentor hanging over the fence, I got nothing but support from Bill Joye. We fell one game short of being 5–5 our first year out. Ironically, we got beat by my old employer, Bartlett Yancey from Caswell County, by my former players. But it was okay; we improved from the year's previous record and continued to improve thereafter.

Wrestling at Graham had been pretty poor ever since my sophomore year in high school. With great determination, I set out to fix it. By doing many fund-raisers, we raised enough money to go to the same wrestling camp I had attended in high school. After all, it had worked for me. So the task began. Camp time arrived with required attendance, and everybody went. They had worked hard in those fund-raisers. Upon arrival at the camp, we had long days of instruction with early-to-bed and early-to-rise schedules. By the end of the week, we were starting to get on each other's nerves, but we won a bunch of matches in the tournament and learned a lot of wrestling maneuvers to go with it.

Oh, by the way, did I mention that we took an old friend, the Mule, on the mountain trip to Appalachian? Or should I say she took us? We threw a mattress in the back, and about twelve or fifteen future stars climbed up into the truck bed for the three-and-a-half-hour mountain journey.

About six of our wrestlers won the individual tournament, so I knew the foundation had been laid. The next fall, we won the conference championship, and I snagged my first Coach of the Year award. But much more was to be done. The following year would be very formative. I had continued to strive to go to wrestling camp, this time at Pembroke State University in Pembroke, North Carolina. We needed another fund-raiser, so this time we contracted to paint an elderly couple's downtown Graham home. It was a very challenging undertaking.

The house was three stories high, and the wood was pretty dilapidated. Once again, everyone had to participate—it was mandatory. The tuition for this camp was over $2,000, just as the one at Appalachian had been.

This house painting was quite a physical undertaking. One of the kids who came from a more well-to-do family asked a question while we were painting the house. He had a bucket and a brush in one hand while preparing to climb the ladder to take him to the top with his other hand. Just before he stepped on the first rung of the ladder, he said, "Coach, I've got all my money for camp, why do I have to paint?"

I pointed to two of his teammates as they came around the side of the house carrying paint cans and brushes. "Do they have their money to go to camp?"

He replied, "I don't think so."

"If they get beat on match night, does it affect you?"

He responded, "Well, yeah."

I said, "So get going and be careful up there."

With a big smile, he began to climb, looking down to monitor his steps. He replied respectfully, "Coach, you're crazy."

We won the conference championship and the Eastern Regional championship and many others. Success had finally arrived. The work ethic we had preached about had rubbed off and worked. We continued to be successful throughout the next two years. With all-state competitors like Brian Turner, Billy Warren, Donnel Farrington, Ralph Hapacheff, Lonnie Thompson, Jeff Liveis, and Dee Hall, Graham was certainly the team of the '80s. This is self-proclaimed. It was recognized by others.

Bartlett Yancey had been called the team of the '70s, with stars like Nelson Watkins, Gary Koger, Vincent Carter, Vernon Reynolds, Sidney Fuqua, Jody Pruitt, Rodrick Henderson, Mitchell England, and George Bigelow.

Would there be a team of the '90s? Yes, but they would wait in the wings awhile. During my time back at Graham, I rekindled many old friendships and developed some lifelong relationships. One of the student teachers from the eastern side of the county did his tenure at Graham. Mr. Glenn Terrel would become a good friend and championship coach at his alma mater, Eastern Alamance, in times after he departed his student teaching at Graham High.

My grandfather died during my return to Graham, and shortly thereafter, my family sold the farm. Suddenly, all the reasons I had come home for were gone. I moved into Graham proper for sixteen years, a stay which was very difficult for the first several years. After all the years I'd slept with the windows open, having peaceful country sounds, I now had to contend with sirens, dogs barking, car horns, people yelling, etc. It took quite a bit of getting used to.

But the farm boy in me never left. I mean, how many city people have two tractors in the backyard, two old pickup trucks, and a yard full of farm equipment? Well, for quite a few years, it was country comes to town on Oakley Street in Graham, North Carolina.

I got real lucky though. If any of you are a country person, you can imagine what it's like to move to a city street anywhere. The people surrounding me were personable. It turned out to be one of the quietest city neighborhoods I've ever been in.

Now, right about here is where the story starts to take a nasty turn. Here I am, living in the city, without the farm and both of my inspirations and main supporters dead. My friend Jim Mach left the head football position he had when he had hired me. He headed to eastern North Carolina, leaving for greener pastures.

Every familiar thing in my life had disappeared all at one time. Everything had changed so fast. I decided to change with it. A friend I made while coaching wrestling at Graham High was then-wrestling coach Jay Perdue, a guy that would become a friend for life as well.

While I was coaching against Coach Perdue, he informed me that there was going to be an opening at Western Alamance, just across the county. So then and there, I began my deliberation whether to leave Graham High School or stay put. After all, I had much success up to this point, record-wise, that is. But at this early age, I still really didn't have a grasp as of yet on all the other good I was doing.

For example, several of the young men who had worked for me kept from getting bored and possibly out of trouble. Others used the money to buy items that they desired but otherwise couldn't afford. Then there were a few who needed these jobs to help their families get by, especially single-parent homes with more than one child.

At this point, I had yet to understand the ways in which success can be measured. A young man named Jeff came out for wrestling his freshman year. Jeff had a leg that had been injured severely at birth. It didn't seem to bother him physically, and he informed me that he wanted to wrestle. He had a doctor's physical okaying him to participate, but I still was very concerned. He also told me he wanted to play football. From my observations, his mobility and speed were limited. He also needed a brace at times to function. I have never in my life discouraged a young person from participating in athletics. However, for his own safety in this case, I did. The young man had had several operations already, and I feared an injury would be forthcoming.

I finally convinced him that he should be the manager for football and wrestling. He accepted, so Jeff became one of the most beloved and influential figures in our athletics program for the rest of his high school career. After explaining his responsibilities in both sports and showing him only one time what to do, he had it. We never had to ask if the travel bags got packed or the uniforms got washed. It automatically took all the pressure off us.

During his third year in high school, we attended wrestling camp at A.C. Reynolds High School in Asheville. Jeff wanted to go along, so I talked to the coaches hosting the camp into allowing Jeff to be the camp trainer. After all, our guys had gotten so used to him taking care of them, they would go straight to him with all their taping problems and minor injuries. He really took care of everybody on both teams, even the coaches.

During this trip to wrestling camp at Asheville, on two separate occasions, the guys involved in the camp had to hike up steep hills, which were a part of a nature walk that was connected to camp. This would have been impossible for Jeff to do but interfered with his desire to do everything the wrestlers did. So the coach hosting the camp put Jeff on his back, piggyback style, and ran up the steep hills whenever they came to one. What a terrific guy. When I arrived to pick up the wrestlers, Jeff informed me of how the coach had helped him up the inclines. I felt it imperative that I thank him. When I did, he replied with, "I couldn't have got along without him. He did everything, I didn't have to ask him." I explained to him it was the same way at home. You wanted to help Jeff, not because of his minor disability, but because he had done so much for you and the team. And as I have said before, the guys on the team loved him. After all, he took care of them. Maybe even more importantly, they respected him.

Jeff was admired not only for his work ethic but an enthusiastic sense of humor. I never saw this young man when he wasn't smiling. This was a lesson a lot of us older folks could manage to learn.

On one funny occasion, our good old successful wrestling team at Graham High was hosting another team scrimmage in our wrestling room there at school. Although the room was rather large, we still had pretty tight quarters. We had four matches going on at one time within those padded walls. One kid missed a maneuver from one of the other teams and hit his head on the wall. After checking him out, I discovered that he was all right; just an ice bag for his head would probably do the trick.

So I sent our trusted wrestling manager with a key to a building where the ice machine was kept. After what seemed a lengthy period, and while the guy with the bump on his head waited on Jeff to return, he came back with no ice. I asked, "Where's the ice?" He said he couldn't get the key to work. Now I would have gone back with him so we could speed things up, but I had to referee.

We got tired of waiting, and the guy with his bump seemed to want to finish his match and took a break sitting along the wall. What seemed to be a long time later, Jeff returned with the ice.

He asked, "Where did the guy go?"

I replied, "He died of old age."

Everybody, including Jeff, started laughing out loud. I looked right at Jeff and said, "I love you, man."

He said, "I love you too," while laughing, "sometimes."

This is what I am talking about. Successes are measured in so many ways that sometimes we just have to look to find them, and other times, they hit us right in the face. Jeff went on to be a very successful man in a community far away. But he is still involved in wrestling, and his is still a remarkable success story. When coaching or teaching, remember they are all worthwhile; the only problem is there's only so much energy a coach or teacher has. This makes it imperative that we all work together toward the same goals without jealousy or preconceived notions that "only my way works." I discovered a long time ago certain teachers and certain coaches reach certain kids while other kids respond to other types of coaches or teachers.

Sometimes, just interacting with other people can give you a totally different outlook on life. For example, I have a three-tiered large trophy case in my house that goes down the living room wall. It's filled with trophies, memorabilia, and pictures of kids and championships of long ago. One of my friends was visiting one day when he started to look inside my trophy cases and exclaimed, "Man, this is one of the most awesome things I've ever seen."

While standing in the kitchen, I asked, "What?"

And he said, "All of these trophies." He then went on to explain that it wasn't the number of trophies there, but it was that for each one of those trophies, it represented thirty to forty lives which were changed in a positive way. I have never thought of it that way. I just kept sticking them in there and giving them an occasional glance as I went by. It's a shame that we get so busy looking ahead in life, sometimes we can't mellow out and look where we've been. Or is it sometimes too painful to remember where we've been?

So now back to where the story begins my dilemma. Do I leave my alma mater and go with my new friend Jay Perdue to Western Alamance? After all, as I mentioned earlier, things had changed so much in my life that many of the things I had come home for were not even there anymore. So with a heavy heart, I left Graham High and went to Western Alamance High. I made several new friends, and guess what, my old college coach, Mickey Brown, was now the head football coach at Western.

It was a different kind of homecoming. This year would be successful coaching-wise, but some more bad luck was on the way. During football practices that year, I had become dizzy, short of breath, and weak. I began to lose energy but just kinda blew it off and kept on plugging away. I got to work with a lot of outstanding folks at Western such as my old friends Mickey Brown, Jay Perdue, and Greg Hill.

At the end of the school year, we had a new superintendent arrive who had the idea that teachers, principals, and coaches should be moved around each year to different schools. Perhaps it was for reasons like the need to break up the "buddy system," or so they called it. Guess who got moved? That's right. I had to go to cross-county Eastern Alamance. Little did I know that by leaving good old Graham High, that my coaching and teaching career would jump on a carousel ride, and it would take me awhile to get it stopped. Eastern Alamance High School would be my next adventure.

But something major was on the way. The dizziness, weakness, and shortness of breath would worsen. I said little or nothing to most but now had developed numbness and a horrific pain in my right arm and elbow. Don't worry, right, I told myself, it's only once in a while.

I knew I needed to go get it checked out, so I did. On a Saturday appointment with a referral from my family doctor, I saw a prominent cardiologist in nearby Greensboro. By this time, I'm in my late thirties and healthy, or so I thought.

After a battery of tests, I sat on an examining room table waiting for a verdict, and the doctor returned and informed me of the problem. He said I had cardiomyopathy.

I asked, "What's that?"

He produced an x-ray of a large white ball.

I asked him what it was, and he said, "It's your heart." He informed me, "Cardiomyopathy is a condition where your heart became so enlarged that it doesn't function as a proper pump."

I asked him what I could have done to cause it, and he said from the evidence, probably pneumonia.

I had had a bad cold that had lasted for about a month or six weeks. You know the type, a deep chest cold. I had gone to my family doctor, and he gave me some antibiotics, but the pneumonia left my heart permanently weakened. This is why I had the shortness of breath.

He then laid down the shocker, "You've got about a year and a half to live."

I was stunned. I began to put on my shirt while he wrote me a prescription. The doctor asked if I had anything to say. I replied, "Don't start digging the hole yet." He laughed and asked me to please take this seriously.

Now headed home with my death sentence, I began to contemplate what was ahead and made a promise that I'd not adversely let it affect my life. How's the coaching/ teaching going, you ask? Well, I didn't miss one single day of work because of my ailment. As a matter of fact, I had accumulated three-hundred and eighty-six sick days by the end of my forty years of teaching and coaching adventures. Not bad for an old man pulling fourteen-hour days in two different sports while teaching multiple subjects, and don't forget the tree business.

By now, my parents were getting older and, being the only child, did my best to help them as time went on. With all my other duties and now this ailment, I began to relate to that old country song by Skeeter Davis, "Stop the World, I Want to Get Off."

Now at Eastern Alamance, I made friends like John Kirby and many others. We had a very successful season in football, making the playoffs and coaching a talented bunch of kids.

The heart condition had gotten no worse or better. Then one night, while watching TV and suffering for several days, I saw a procedure on *60 Minutes* called ventricular remodeling. These doctors at the Cleveland Clinic in Ohio cut a piece from your heart to make it smaller, therefore allowing it to be a more efficient pump. I called a few days later and made an appointment. I drove myself up to Ohio for another battery of tests, and I was asked a bunch of questions. After all, I didn't look sick, I certainly wasn't a threat to them, and I never hurt or even missed a day of work.

After an overnight visit and that battery of tests we discussed, the doctor (Hobbs) who had perfected this method, it was decided that I was a perfect candidate for the procedure. He also explained how he had gotten this procedure from an Arab doctor who performed the surgery in a tent.

Of course, here comes the "good" part again. He informed me that there was a good risk involved as well. Many patients who had gone through the surgery were leading active lives. On the other hand, others had gotten worse. On the all-day ride home, I had plenty of time to think. Once that piece of tissue is gone, you can't put it back, and though I suffered some, I was still very functional. I decided to keep taking my medication and leave well enough alone.

In the meantime, I did not let my coaching career get stagnant. I was offered a job as a science teacher and defensive co-coordinator at Mt. Tabor High School in Winston-Salem, North Carolina. My old high school wrestling coach Harold Smith was assistant principal and got the authority to offer me this job.

This brought on more decisions. Winston-Salem was sixty-five miles one way. My parents were older now and still living on part of the farm. I couldn't afford to move. Therefore, I'd have to commute if I were to take the job. Once again, I would throw caution to the wind. So here me and my old friend, the Mule, with hundreds of thousands of miles on her, would drive every day back and forth to Winston-Salem. I made some more lasting friends like Oscar Brayboy, the head football coach, and of course, my high school wrestling coach Harold Smith was there.

With my new position as defensive coordinator and science teacher, I now had experience successfully coaching at every classification. This school was in the 4-A metro league. To my surprise, it was no different that 1-A, 2-A, or 3-A. You just had a lot more kids. My heart was fine as long as I took my medication. I'd get up in the morning for summer practice and arrive at Mt. Tabor at nine, practice to eleven, and then return via the hour or so commute home. I thought to myself, *This isn't too bad.* After all, at this time in history, gas wasn't too high yet.

One day before practice, Coach Brayboy had a meeting with the fellow coaching staff. He made the comment, "When school begins in another week, we will begin practice at 2:30 PM.

I asked immediately, "What time do we get out of school?"

He said 2:00 PM.

Then I asked, "I know I don't want to ask this question. What time do we begin school?"

He replied, "7:20 AM."

What was left of my already-messed-up heart sank. This would make for an ordinary day of getting up at 5:00 AM, getting on the road at 6:00 AM, and getting home on an average night at 7:00 PM. This didn't count game nights. Sometimes I would go to work at 6:00 AM and roll in at 1:00 AM the next morning. Thank God, the next morning was Saturday.

I loved Winston-Salem, but as you could imagine, this sixty-five-mile all-day everyday job began to take its toll. After all, I still had the wood business and elderly parents. You're probably thinking, "And you wonder why you have heart problems."

So after this year and a successful stint as defensive coordinator at Mt. Tabor, I realized I had to get closer to home. After all, we were the number one defensive unit in the area in 4-A. I was offered many jobs with the same title in and around Winston-Salem. I was even asked to stay on in Winston-Salem, but the hometown was calling. I didn't know how close I could get, but I had to try.

I guess you're beginning to wonder if I could hold a job. Well, let's put it this way. I've been asked back at one time or another to take jobs at all the schools I've worked at plus some others. My grandfather had told me one time, if you can go back where you've been and get a job, then you did an excellent job when you were there.

I went on a job search and found one in Durham where I coached at Southern Durham High School for a year. We were once again very successful, but here, as in Winston-Salem, I had been exposed to inner-city students, gangs and clannish behavior, with high crime rates perpetrated mainly on themselves. Many times, I'd have two different gangs in my classroom glaring at each other, aware that they had been fighting on the streets just hours before. It's really sad to see sometimes what we as adults or as a society for that matter can do to kids.

In Durham, I was one of only three white teachers in the school. Therefore, expectations of an all-black student body were different. How do I mean? One day, before class began, after I'd been there several months, a student in one of my classrooms stood up and said, "You know, you are a pretty cool dude."

My response was, "Thank you, but what makes you arrive at that conclusion?"

He replied, "When we first saw you in here wearing those cowboy boots, dress shirts, and driving that monster truck, we thought we had us a 'neck. But you really care whether we learn or not."

I replied, "I sure do, and when I don't care anymore, I'm hanging up my chalk and whistle." Thank God that day hasn't ever arrived.

I proceeded to ask him and his fellow classmates what the word *stereotype* meant. One of the brighter female students answered, "That's when one thing appears to be one thing, but overconditioning it could be something totally different."

My reply was, "You weren't sleeping after all."

Many laughed. I explained to them I once heard a great motivational speech by a black man, who told the following story. Once, while giving a speech to an auditorium of mixed students, by mixed, I mean black, white, Asian, etc., he was trying to get them revved up for the upcoming school year and had been asked to come to this school and speak to them for this purpose.

While giving his speech, he noticed a tall long-haired slovenly dressed white boy sitting on the front row. He looked as though he could use a bath, but the very worst thing was he talked off and on during the entire speech. Who did he think he was? The dynamic speaker thought, *This white boy is totally disrespecting me, probably because I'm black, he thinks I have nothing important to say.* He finished his speech and stood in the foyer of the auditorium as well-wishers and students filed by. All of a sudden, this slovenly dressed, bath-needing, inattentive young man approached him, hand held out for a shake, and he said, "Dr. Harrison, really enjoyed your speech. I heard everything you said in there, and I'm ready for the new school year. Come back soon."

All of a sudden, the ugly head of racism had reared its ugly head again (my own). I went on to share with these students this story and others in reverse. One student said, "You don't expect to pull us in with that sappy story, do you?"

"No, but you didn't go to sleep, did you?"

I enjoyed teaching, as many people don't, in those inner-city schools. A teacher is a teacher whether standing on a soapbox on a sidewalk, in front of a fancy, expensive podium, or somewhere in a large auditorium. And contrary to widespread belief, coaching is just an extension of the teaching day.

I made many new friends in Durham, some are dead now, but some like Pete Shankle and others seem to be ageless. I was chosen to attend a teaching fellowship at Duke University in the earlier '90s. They only selected a handful of teachers from throughout the state, and I was honored. The area I was assigned was Lupus. Since I was sort of a science/PE buff, I got a kick out of it.

One day, while sitting in my classroom, I had kept a student in for misbehaving in class. While he was sitting there reading a book, my cell phone rang. It was my old friend, Jay Perdue. He was at Cummings High School in Burlington, NC (home), and said the athletic director and head football coach wanted to talk with me. I asked what about. He replied, "You'll have to talk with him." I set up an appointment with head coach Steve Johnson. I had no idea of what an adventure I was about to embark upon.

In the meantime, life went on in the teachings of the inner city. One day, after class was over, I had stared around for about an hour for any student who would bother to come by and ask for extra help in class or whatever. The door opened, and several members of the local street gang were standing there. They closed the door and said, "You've been leaning on us too much in class. You've been expecting us to be like everybody else, and we're not like anybody else. We are the Crips, and we don't answer to anybody, especially to a white motherfucker like you."

So I stood up and asked, "Okay, so what's up?"

The leader of the group said, "I am going to watch while my posse beats you down, then I am going to spit on you."

My reply, they could not believe. I stood at my desk and said, "Okay," as I rolled up my sleeves, "Let's get with it."

The leader exclaimed, "You're not scared, are you?"

I said, "No, I've dealt with punks like you all my life. It's nothing new. I grew up very rough, so there's nothing you can do to me or say to me that's going to change the way I feel, and hopefully whatever I say will someday change the way you look at things. So let's get with it. You came here for a fight, and I sure don't want to disappoint you."

The leader said, "There's five of us and one of you."

I replied, "Oh, that's all right. There are enough of you to do what you came here to do to me. But when it starts, I'm gonna grab one of you, and when he's through, while the rest of you do whatever you want to me, I'll have my hands on one of you, and that guy isn't gonna get loose. You guys came here for a fight, so let's get at it."

With my lack of fear, it seemed to defeat their purpose. They looked very bewildered. They walked out of my classroom without saying a word. I was just as perplexed as they were. I guess their threats and intimidation had carried them for most of their lives. Or all of a sudden, all that street savvy didn't work simply because they ran upon an individual for whom personal safety didn't matter. They couldn't comprehend it. An individual that had been through so much physical and emotional pain that whatever damage they might do would only be minor. They all showed up in class on a regular basis with little or no incident for the rest of the year.

There were two beautiful black girls who carried themselves way ahead of the rest of us that came to class every day. They were excellent students who, like the gang members, would appear one afternoon in that hour I stayed after class.

Both of them were honor students, so when they entered the room, after the normal amenities, I asked, "What are you two young ladies doing here?"

One of them began a spiel, "We thought we needed to come by and talk to you before something happens to you."

I replied, "That's great, but why would you all be worried about me?"

One of those young and beautiful women said, "We love you and respect you, but you are out of your league."

So I replied, "Why would you say that?"

"These people are street thugs, and they don't care about learning anything. You just gave them some new rules they can defy. They'll kill you if they have to."

My response was, "Don't worry, I've already been warned by them."

They looked at me, perplexed, and left the room with nothing but hope and well-wishes. Just before they left, I said, "Whatever you do, don't give up on those thugs, yourself, and especially me."

They left with big smiles, with one of them exclaiming, "That crazy white boy." During our conversation, the other young woman asked, "Coach, are you crazy?"

So here will come my conflict for the future. No greater difficult coaching or teaching experience have I ever had than while I was teaching in the inner-city schools of Durham, North Carolina.

That black/white tension fueled by years of racial troubles made whatever you said or did be taken with a grain of salt. The only thing that could have overcome it would be years of placement in the community, hence the conflict. I wanted to go home.

CHAPTER 7

Appreciation

I feel like anyone who teaches in the inner-city schools, especially if they're white, is doing a deed so much greater than themselves, no one could speak to. A principal at one of the inner-city schools where I taught and coached at called me in one day for a chat. Of course, I thought I was in trouble, only to be informed at how pleased he was with my performance. His first words were, "Color doesn't matter to you, does it?"

I said, "We are referring to the students and me being the only white thing in sight?"

He replied, "Exactly."

"I don't see color, only hope and expectations."

He replied, "They see it as well. Do you know how many phone calls I've had about that white teacher in my school, making individuals work and giving them hope?"

I replied, "I've always done what I was hired to do. My job is to teach."

He responded, "Teachers are great motivators and performers and, Mr. Hawks, you certainly are that. The community is watching. Good work and keep it up."

And with this, the conflict within myself became greater. I wanted to go home, but this forty-five-minute commute and the difficulty of the lives of the students I was helping were so challenging for a humanitarian like myself; the choice would become a very onerous task. How do you influence some who still have a lot of work to do? Those two lovely girls who were students of mine would appear later on in my life.

I'll let you keep reading. I know I don't believe it either after coaching Southern Durham to many championships. It was time for me to go home. Now that I was trying to come home, the call from Cummings seemed to be destiny. However, I was in a dilemma over feeling like I had to leave an area where I'd probably done the most good in my entire teaching career. But that was very noticeable due to the much bigger problem. Until we get the state's educational problems solved and that being that, we just can't throw money at the problem, that we should all receive equal money for schools, and until we get over the problem with overspending, then try to work back in the one area which is education, we are going to flounder.

Later on, some of those participants who had done so much with nothing will be discussed, and I would be very honored to be recognized among that group. A great conflict would begin within myself. I felt as if I'd probably done the most good wherever I'd taught. Don't get me wrong. I didn't feel like the great white hope either. But that pull to come home still lingered.

After one interview with Coach Steve Johnson from Cummings High School, I decided to come home. After all, there was a ten-minute drive to work, compared to a forty-five-minute commute. Plus, all my friends of the past were here on the same staff. I'd pretty much been offered the job, so I tendered my resignation with Durham public schools, and I must say, I had many regrets. The conflict was great.

Many would see it as a no-brainer. Drive a long way to help students or drive ten minutes to do the same thing. My hometown loyalty won out.

Now we'd find out if Cummings would be the team of the '90s as mentioned earlier. At Cummings, much like the Durham public schools, I had a talented group of athletes to recruit from. I began immediately upon my arrival to recruit for wrestling, from my ninth-grade biology classes and my JV football team of which I was the head coach. After all, the sooner they began to get their feet wet, the sooner they would develop as individuals.

When I first began teaching at Cummings in the classroom, the teachers made up the final exams. So we all knew exactly what we had taught, and that's ultimately what the students were tested on. Easy, right? It would change very shortly. After all, I was an unheard-of commodity, a biology/earth science/physical science/physical education/health teacher/coach, who was certified in all these areas.

I was also someone who could and would coach football and wrestling and take on other noninstructional duties. What do I mean? Well, lunchroom duty, hall duty, bathroom watch, parking lot duties, prom chaperone, homecoming dance chaperone, appearing at cultural events, etc. Anyone who ever thought a teacher was paid too much just needs to shadow one for a few days, with that teacher's permission, of course. I've taught in roughly eight different high schools in North Carolina over the past thirty years, and I can honestly say there are very, very few bad teachers. However, since they are so in the public spotlight, it brings cries of outrage anytime one gets brought to attention by the media. You know the deal, like the reaction to a teacher who's broken the public's trust or how the law reflects on us all. We seemingly are all viewed as disgraced by our colleague's sins. Now, don't get me wrong. I don't mind getting held to a high grade of accountability. After all, I held one of the most important positions in the civilized world. I mean, I grew up in a household where it was preacher, teacher, and doctor in rank of importance to civilization. The teaching of young people is one of the most important, if not the most important, job in the world.

Many believe, as I do, that a teacher owes their students a lot more knowledge than just what's in that textbook of their assigned course of study. Students want to know about the practical application of what they are expected to learn. Or more simply, how they were going to be able to use it or apply it to future endeavors.

Once they've come to that realization, they buy into what you are trying to do more easily. Don't get me wrong. They don't all buy into it each time, but eventually they do. Motivational techniques vary from teacher to teacher, but the educators who make the class fun have the best success. I know, who cares if they're entertained while they learn? (The students do.) Don't get me wrong. Even the best laid plans by many skillful teachers who have taught many classes before may occasionally flop. So they must have a backup plan.

Upon my arrival at Cummings, we had a program that had been there for many years and had been quite successful. Then, under the new No Child Left Behind educational plan, adopted by all the states in the United States, after a questionably successful tenure in Texas, all stability began to crumble. Students were held to accountability that I'm not sure anyone could master.

The state of North Carolina had to adopt the plan, and all other states were falling in line. The pressure became intense. Teachers began teaching to the End of Course Test instead of the curriculum, so a lot of the practicality and relevance went out the window. Schools began to be labeled "low performing" or "at standard" or "school of excellence," according to the results of the End of Course Test.

The End of Course Test was written by the state. A body of veteran teachers, who had compiled their experiences of what they thought would be expected of a college workload, wrote tests preparing students for this. At first, the state sent out curriculum guides when we still had teacher-made tests, where you utilize what you had taught from the text for the final exams. Now the state sent out an objective sheet on what was to be specifically taught, and everyone passed the finals. Wonderful, right?

Large bonuses were given to schools who met expected growth or were excellent while the ones that were labeled "low performing" just got ridiculed, shamed, embarrassed by the media, and very critical teams were put in the schools to intervene.

As time went on, the blame game continued. Oh, yeah, no matter what, it was always the teachers, the parents, or someone else. Just not the state. No one wanted to admit the real problem was with the "new" curriculum standards. Some of the kids had gotten this far without the proper skills to survive. They had just been passed. The real problem was they wanted to succeed, wanted to learn, but sadly, for the most part, a lot of them couldn't read. It wasn't just in my school and the other North Carolina schools but many other states across the country. A new "expert" came in and set up a reading mediation course. The real problem, after all, was that the students couldn't understand the questions once they read them, and you couldn't do anything to help them understand either.

So they answered what they could, becoming quickly frustrated and just began to bubble in answers randomly. You know the bubble-in test, right? Where some of the choices for answers include A of the above, B of the above, A and B of the above, C of the above, C and D of the above, all of the above, or none of the above. Wait a minute, what was the question anyway? With months of remedial reading, our test scores slowly rose, and with it, our students' respect of themselves, their teachers, and their schools.

Most of it happened because questions were asked of the veteran teachers who responded with a workable solution. After all, if the classroom teacher doesn't know why they're failing, who does? A student in my class once made a derogatory remark about the school while looking right at me and just loud enough for me to hear it. My quick response was, "Quit talking about yourself like that."

He asked, "Myself?"

I replied, "Yeah, and myself and him too," pointing to a student on the front row.

The student asked, "What are you taking about?"

My reply was, "When you say something negative about the school, you're taking about all your friends, myself, all the other teachers, and yourself."

He asked, "How do you mean?"

I said, "We are in this school, all of us, so we are in this thing together. Low rating, high rating, it's all on us."

The student responded, "I've never thought about it like that before," and I replied, "That's why I'm here, to make you think."

There's nothing more humiliating than to have your school blamed when you know your students are embarrassed by some label that's been placed on them. But to their credit, they, along with the help of their highly qualified teachers, rated among the finest schools in the state.

Adversity in life will do only two things. It will bring you and your teammates together or drive you apart. You'll have to be the ones to decide which it's going to be. This faculty came closer together and remains that way still today. Some ten years later, oh, yeah, we still have some slumps in those End of Course Tests, but they don't last very long.

Now that it seems like we have the academic problems on the run, let's buckle back up to the athletics.

Cummings High School, since its inception in 1970, has developed a rich athletic tradition, with many sports. There was a reputation to live up to, and I was with just the people to do it. After all, on one of the T-shirts head coach Steve Johnson designed to give each player on our football team, and each one of the coaches can be seen on the next page front and back. I know you're gonna ask that question, "Coach, are you crazy?"

IF YOU THINK YOU'RE AS GOOD AS CUMMINGS

THINK AGAIN !

1988 STATE CHAMPS
1989 EASTERN REGIONAL CHAMPS
1990 STATE CHAMPS
1992 STATE CHAMPS
1993 EASTERN REGIONAL CHAMPS

MID-STATE CHAMPS

1977	1987	1990
1979	1988	1991
1986	1989	1993

1994...WHAT DO YOU THINK ?

I bet you are wondering by now, what about the heart condition? Well, along about this time in my life in the '90s, I felt a little worse some days but nothing debilitating. Remember, I had three hundred and eighty-three sick days upon retirement. The men that I would spend the rest of my coaching career with, at least up to that point, were like brothers, and if you ask any one of them separately, they'll tell you the same thing. Coach Steve Johnson, who'd really play a big part in my life (later), would hire me to teach me his organizational skills and would constantly flash brilliance as a former defensive coordinator for some of those championships I mentioned earlier, all the while leading us as an entire group closer toward our common goal. He would also serve as athletic director in my earlier years at Cummings, all the while I taught biology in the classroom. Still think teachers make enough money?

Then there was Coach Frank Mensch, a wacky, loveable, fix-anything-that-would-break type of guy. He was knowledgeable on defense and was an excellent position coach. I'm talking about any position on defense. He was a man who the kids loved and had been my friend since high school. When Cummings was in its fledgling stages in the 1970s and was playing just about all ninth and tenth graders on their varsity team, I was in high school at good ol' Graham High. We would play Cummings in all sports quite frequently. Coach Mensch would always be my cheerleader in football and wrestling.

He could yell out, "Hey, Hawks, excellent job, young 'un," which brought smiles from everybody within hearing distance. He was a dear friend and fellow coach for almost forty years later. Little did I know in 1973 that in 1977, I would return to Cummings, not as a Graham athlete, but as a student teacher in PE. Yep, you guessed it. Coach Frank Mensch would be my supervising teacher at Hugh M. Cummings High School, my future home for umpteen years. I am very sincere as I speak of this man because as the initial draft of this book was being written, he was undergoing neck surgery to fuse damaged vertebra, probably left over from Elon University playing days. My prayers were with him, and he came out just fine.

Next on the list of fellow coaches is my old friend Coach Jay Perdue. Remember the former offensive coordinator at Western Alamance and former wrestling coach at the same school? By now, he had played a role in leading almost all the wins mentioned on the T-shirt on the previous pages. He had also played a key role in eighteen state championships, either as an assistant or as a head coach. Coach Donnie Davis at Cummings has probably won more in track that anyone else in NC history. He and Coach Jay Perdue together have accomplished what most coaches only dream of. Over the years, Coach

Perdue has become a close personal friend, one I have come to cherish.

Then there is Coach Eddie Foust, a gentle giant, at least most of the time. He was one of my fellow classmates at Elon University, although he and Coach Brent Shepherd are right much older than me. These dear friends would later play a part in my life that could not be equaled. Not just Coach Foust or Coach Shepherd, but all these champions. No, we are not there yet, but later.

Coach Isley, the offensive line coach and a Southern Alamance product along with Mike Johnson, both Southern Alamance alums, would also be important influences on the outcome of our seasons. Both varsity and JV football teams would begin to prosper. Then Coach Danny McCauley would arrive, the youngest member of our staff who would catch up quickly, with much knowledge and effectiveness.

Coach George Robinson Jr. would also play an integral part in our football program. Over the years, he also won several championships in varsity men's basketball. Several more folks came in and out of our program over the years but never stayed long. It seemed the older we got, the harder we all worked. The young coaches just didn't seem to want to keep up.

Kim Annas, a basketball coach who won Cummings's first basketball state championship with Coach George

Robinson as his assistant, was my roommate for a while, then moved on to become very successful in the Durham public schools as a coach and administrator.

One day, we were coaching football on one of those hot August afternoon sessions, and a young man approached me from behind the baseball back stop. A well-groomed, energetic, confident individual who was a minister, teacher, and basketball coach, it was Coach Annas. Not only was he a unique combination, but so were the both of us. The next four years would be interesting. As he moved in with me in my small home in Graham, North Carolina, he would become a dear friend, roommate, and skilled basketball coach. All still in place today except for the roommate part.

It seems so easy to talk about all these outstanding men who have dedicated their lives to the young people, not only of North Carolina but of the world. The people of North Carolina don't know what they've missed if they haven't made the acquaintance of these special men. No, I'm not biased, just convinced. If you had seen them as I have, day in and day out, working with athletes that were highly talented and some not so much, you'd know what I meant. All these men exemplify the word *coach*, which to me is almost a holy word, knowing what it entails. Some think you can hang a whistle around almost anyone's neck and yell "coach," and that's perfectly all right. Not me, however. I'm so old now I've almost come full circle.

I find myself going up against coaches that are younger and younger. Sometimes, now don't get me wrong, it's hard to tell them from the kids by appearance. On some occasions, I've even had the opportunity to coach against individuals who I've actually coached.

You really have to mind your p's and q's when you play those guys because they would like nothing better than to beat their mentor. All that doesn't matter in the least, not to this old man. As long as they do things the right way, win or lose, it doesn't matter.

What do you mean about the right way, you say? I mean by putting the kids first. By learning all you can about the sport you're coaching, the benefits of what's best for the kids is more important than winning an athletic contest. You set an example by your own behavior and expect your athletes to do the same. And always let them know even if it's only through our actions, that *you care*, not just whether they win or lose, but how they succeed as people.

You're thinking, gosh, that's a lot to remember. Not really. Well, maybe in the beginning when you're kinda green, but after a while, if you'll just be yourself, as it was with me, it will come. It's kinda like life. It'll come naturally. Never put up barriers as to who you are, not just to the kids, but with anyone in your life. You'll miss out on a great deal if you do.

For the most part, I've been very proud of my associations with students that have gone into coaching and teaching as I did. Many return to ask advice, and I merely refer to the guidelines I had laid out in the previous paragraphs. On occasion, you'll have to correct some who have misinterpreted that the kids are first, and nothing else matters. Many times, the young coach, full of himself or herself, let winning creep up on the scale of importance to equality of well-being or sometimes surpassing it. As I've indicated before, you take care of the kids first, and the winning will take care of itself. However, being successful is important too. That's what keeps them coming out, sells tickets, and in some cases, secures your job. If you are willing to risk losing an athletic contest by sitting out a couple of players who broke the team rules by missing practice, etc., in order to make a point with the team, then you know what I'm talking about.

Surrounded with all these dear friends, some former rivals and now colleagues, Cummings's athletic fortunes began the mid-'90s with great hope and anticipation. The 1990s were very successful for us and me personally. I glowed in the limelight of success one year and fell like a rock the next. In 1995, our JV football and wrestling enjoyed success, so as usual, the summer of 1995, we decided to take the wrestling team to camp. Southwest Randolph County offered a $70 per player, one-week camp at their school in a neighboring county. So after another fund-raiser, we began our trek through the county one beautiful summer morning in July to attend this weeklong camp. The first day on session was pretty uneventful. I was pleased with our wrestlers' performance and so were the other coaches attending, as we discussed our team's athleticism. The first session ended with our team reversing our path and heading home through the commute. The athletic director and myself had agreed commuting would be more economical, being it was one county over and only a week.

CHAPTER 8

Another Close Call

The country road on which we traveled was the old Highway 49 from Liberty to Asheboro. I watched the thirteen wrestlers I had on board as they sat at the back of the bus. This was unusual because most of the time on any trip, they sat at the front and carried on conversations with each other. Today, however, they all huddled in the back.

Some asleep, others listening to their headsets, all were quiet on our homeward journey. But not for long, for about halfway between Asheboro and Liberty, we entered a part of the roadway that had a short one-hundred-dred-yard visible stretch that crossed a one-lane bridge, then immediately entered a curve with thick trees on both sides of the road.

Visibility was minimal. Due to the curve, and just as we entered it and were about to exit the old one-lane bridge, suddenly, the unimaginable happened. A 1982 older model Blazer entered the same curve from the other direction, running more than sixty miles per hour and on our side of the road. If I'd have been chewing gum, I'd have swallowed it.

While the large white vehicle appeared to head straight at us, I yelled, "Hang on!" and veered to the right. We knocked off part of the bridge as we left the road, and I turned my head away just before impact, and at that moment, I thought I was gone. By shifting to the right, I had managed to avoid a head-on collision. I was later informed by the investigating highway patrol officer that the wreck probably would have resulted in my student athletes' injury or death had I not angled away. However, we took a broadside hit on the driver's right front passenger door.

Now, I thought I'd been hit in football, but oh, man, what a lick for anyone who's never been hit by something moving sixty miles per hour. I don't recommend it. Believe me. All you bungee jumpers just stick with that. Upon collision, I was knocked out from the driver's seat into the front of the aisle, the windshield shattering, filling my hair with glass and flying debris. The fender and door collapsed, trapping both my legs under the dash while they were still on the pedals. As soon as all the commotion stopped, I thought, *Oh, God, please don't let any of those kids be hurt.* I rolled on my stomach as best I could. My legs were still trapped in the crushed metal on the front of the bus.

It's funny how you remember things after it's all over. I recall thinking right before impact, *Oh my god, those kids*. Even after I had already accepted my own passing, I rolled onto my stomach and yelled, "How many are hurt?" I looked to the back for an answer, and all I saw were foreheads and eyes peering just above the backs of the rear seats. Then one of those remarkable kids yelled, "We're all right, but you're tore up, ain't you?"

I replied, "It's not good." I called for my senior captain to come to the front of the bus, and as he started forward, I could see that he was very upset. My head was busted open, so I took off my coaching shirt, wrapped it around my fist, and compressed it tightly to the open wound.

The bleeding was really bad, and it was blurring my vision. When my captain got to the front, he said, "Oh my gosh, look at your legs, Coach!"

I smelled smoke. His eyes began to well with tears, and I knew he was gonna panic, not only himself but the rest of them. He said, "We're going to burn up."

I reached up, grabbed him by his shirt—that's all I could reach, and pulled him onto the floor with me.

I yelled, "Listen, you pull yourself together. Nobody's gonna burn up or get killed. We've missed that chance," while I smiled looking into his eyes.

He began to partially smile with tears rolling down his cheeks. I told him if he and I panicked, it would put the rest of them in danger. In the meantime, the driver from the other vehicle, a woman, began to scream out uncontrollably, which of course worsened my job.

I instructed him to go to the back, get the uniforms and equipment, and to lead the rest off the bus to a safe area off the road. I knew this would give them something to do while I took on the horrific job of pulling my legs one at a time from the twisted wreckage of the bus, if I could stand the pain or even get them out at all.

I rolled back over, and the gash on my head was beginning to slow down from bleeding for a little bit. With both hands, I pulled one leg at a time from the wreckage. Some of my lower leg bones were sticking out through my pant legs. I couldn't feel my ankles—they didn't respond to movement impulse. When my ankles flopped from side to side uncontrollably and gave the sound of broken glass, I knew not just by appearance I was hurt pretty bad. Pulling those legs from that wreckage was a pain like no other experience I had had in my life.

Once I had them both out, I yelled for the captain and two others to return quickly through the emergency door in the back of the bus and toted me to a safe position already occupied by the other team members on the side of the road. As my wrestlers carried me to a safe distance away from the bus, I instructed them to put me down.

Many days later, I'd wake up to a terrible itch on my entire backside. When I told the doctor in the hospital to take a look, he informed me, "Congratulations, you have a severe case of poison oak."

To which I replied, "My athletic heroes dumped me on the safe haven I'd chosen on the side of the road. Right in a bed of poison oak." Well, they did exactly as they were told.

While we were on the side of the road, I asked my captain to lean over, so I could talk to him. I told him to keep the others at the same distance from me until help arrived. Keep them bunched up there. If they go near the bus, someone may drive through that mess, and they could still get hurt.

I then said, "Speaking of help, anyone got a cell phone?"

One kid said, "Yes," so I told him to call 911 and tell them we needed an ambulance and patrol car on Old 49-A between Liberty and Asheboro. I'd lost mine, but I guess it was still on the bus. The lady in the Blazer frequently called for help but with no legs and these guys to look after, left little I could do. I instructed my captain again to keep them safe on the side of the road until help arrived. I told him it would be dark soon, and the situation would become even more dangerous. I also alerted him that I could pass out due to blood loss, and he'd have to be in charge. He agreed and seemed more worried about me than anything else.

What seemed like an eternity, but just before dark, we heard a siren coming. They put the kids and me in the ambulance, pulled the lady out of the other vehicle, and rushed us all to the hospital. While putting me in the ambulance, one of the highway patrolmen said, "Oh, God, look at your legs, why aren't you screaming out loud?"

I told him if I'd done that, those kids would have panicked and run across six counties. He laughed. He said, "I see what you mean."

I told him, "Besides, if you think yelling and screaming will help, I'll start right now."

The kids called from the hospital in Asheboro, and their parents picked them up. They stayed by my side until all their rides got there, one by one. Once they were all gone, a doctor arrived and introduced himself as an orthopedic surgeon.

He posed the question, "Do you want to try and put your legs back together here, or do you prefer a doctor in Graham or Burlington?"

I requested they ship me back to Burlington so our orthopedic surgeon for Cummings could do the job. I'd seen him do some amazing things with our athletes who had some pretty major injuries.

About that time, tears began to run down my face as I lay on my back in that hospital room, thinking as I looked up, "Thank you, God, for not letting any of those kids get hurt. Thank you."

The doctor looked at me and said, "You seem to be in a lot of pain." But not in as much as you'd expect. He said, "I'll have the nurse give you something before we ship you to Burlington." It's so funny how you think of things at the most uncanny times. When the doctor returned to give me the knockout shot, I was laughing. He kinda half-frowned and half-smiled, asking, "Are you okay?"

I replied, "Yeah, I'm okay."

When I was playing sports in high school and in college and I'd carry my stuff out to the car on my way to a game, my grandmother would ask, "Have you got on clean underwear?" I would reply, "Yes, why?" Then she would say, "If you got hurt in that game and they took you to the hospital and cut off your pants, if you had on dirty underwear, I'd have to leave this country. I'd be so embarrassed."

This ritual continued all through high school. Then came my first college experience with Bluefield State of West Virginia. On the way to the car, my grandmother asked, "Do you have on clean underwear?" I replied, "Yes, why?" This I said before she could reply, "Grandma, who do you know in West Virginia?" We both burst out laughing. She said, "You know what I mean."

So suddenly, as I lay there in Asheboro with my crushed legs and pants almost torn off, I remembered that funny story of my beloved grandma. I looked up at the ceiling as I smiled and said to myself, *They are clean.*

My unsuspecting doctor caught me reminiscing about a somewhat happier time in my life. On my way out, there wasn't much to shield me from all the reporters and camera flashes asking questions and popping. I was heavily sedated so it was all kind of a blur. I was what you would say whisked away, so to speak.

After what seemed to be a short ride back to Burlington, my friends, Coaches Johnson, Perdue, Foust, Robinson, and Shepherd met me at Alamance Regional Medical Center along with a mob of reporters and TV cameras. By now, the newspapers and TV stations were running the story of the crazy coach who was near death. Not really, but you know how those things get exaggerated.

My friends and fellow coaches set up a barrier behind which they could roll my gurney, all dressed in their Cummings's football attire. For the first time, I realized what they meant when they used to tell me after my hiring, "You are now part of a family."

Well-wishers and my immediate family waited with me in a corner of the emergency room as they prepared to examine the severity of my injuries. After heavily sedating me, I was returned from the examining room, and the orthopedic surgeon informed me that both my ankles were crushed, and my bones were broken in both lower legs. Nothing like good news, huh? He then informed me that he would do his best to repair them, but they may be damaged beyond repair.

I told him, "Doc, they didn't leave us much to work with, just do the best you can."

He said he really didn't know how bad it would be until he got in there.

I told him, "Just don't cut anything off until you wake me up and let me know first."

He then took a very serious tone and said, "Andy, I'll do what I can, but your legs are a mess."

"Doc, I'm not going to have a limp, am I?"

He said, "Andy, we've always been friends, so I can't promise you anything. I'm not sure how well you'll walk or even run again."

I said, "Hold on, doc, I wasn't running before the wreck. You just get 'em facing the right direction, and I'll walk again without a limp."

He said, "You sound awfully sure of yourself."

I replied, "I know me."

He said that wreck would have killed the average man. I said that must be true. He was the third person who had told me that. "Doc, I keep telling ya I'm not the average man."

So after heavy consultation with my heart doctor in Chapel Hill, the putting back together of Andy Hawks began for I don't know how many times now. After all, by this point, I'd already had four knee operations in the summers of my freshman and sophomore years of college.

Six more hours (three on each leg) from the ankle down would be required to make me whole again. Talk about the bionic man, I sure wasn't, but it was beginning to feel like it.

When I awoke two days later, I found myself hosting three giant metal rod poles and halos protruding from already-skinny legs. I will exhibit those on some of the upcoming pages; it ain't pretty. The doctor came in to my room and informed me he had replaced my larger lower leg bones with metal rods and halo-type devices at my ankles.

Two wing nuts that now would hold my feet were in place. The doctor almost guaranteed me arthritis in the near future. I thought the worst was over, but now came what was possibly one of the most frustrating things any-one might have to go through in life. A long, patient, demanding, and painful rehabilitation period.

After many months of physical therapy and rehabil-itation, the day would come when I would walk again. However horrifyingly painful it was, I walked, first with the help of a walker, then crutches, and finally, a cane. I remember in the hospital getting up and walking down a ramp, then rising from a wheelchair to walk this path of parallel bars. Those were the first steps I would take. Up until now, I had mostly lay on the floor in my living room on a blanket, scooting myself about the floor. It was great to stand upright again and finally take a hot shower, divorcing all those terrible sponge baths. The world looked different from a wheelchair, believe me. I know it's been said by so many and so many times, but you don't realize how much the things we take for granted mean to us until they are gone. Simple everyday occurrences like walking from one room to another. You become so appreciative once you've had them, lost them, and then slowly regain them again.

It took a lot of hard work, but I made a 98 percent recovery from my sixty-mile-per-hour collision. By 98 percent, I mean I don't walk with a limp. I have limited motion, arthritis, and little joint flexibility and stiffness. But they function, sometimes painfully. So I had kept my bargain with the doctor. Get them back facing the right direction, and I'd walk again.

My fellow coaches, my family, if you will, visited me regularly, giving me encouragement and support on many occasions, and they visited me in the hospital. I'm not sure whether my principal was joking or not, but she inquired, "Do you think you will be able to teach sitting in that wheelchair?"

I quickly replied with a hearty laugh, "There is no way I am going to face a bunch of high school kids while in a wheelchair."

She burst out laughing as well.

After about ten weeks, I was back in the classroom and on the wrestling mat again. I missed football season that year due to my injuries. Two weeks later, I'd be driving a bus again on the way to our first scrimmage of the season. Yep, it was back to business as usual. So I had survived the heart scare (so far) and getting run over by a runaway Blazer. Some would begin to call me lucky while others would grow to believe the opposite. To quote a father of one of my fellow coaches, "Dang, what else is going to happen to that boy?"

My coaching career continued to flourish as my first year back proceeded, and again, we won the conference championship in wrestling. I would become Coach of the Year, one of the fifteen times I had won it in my career.

In the following years, I would be blessed with many wonderful relationships, championships, honors, and some more tragedies. Since I have been talking about 1998 and the wreck, let's talk about a student of mine whom I had taught biology in my classes at Cummings High School that same year. This wonderful student would nominate me to be selected into the Who's Who Among

American Teachers. It would also happen two more times in my teaching career. However, the first time seems so very special somehow, as did the wonderful young lady, Jackie Morton, who had nominated me. Jackie, who now holds a successful position in a large company in a nearby city, would call to check up on me during some tough times down the road. Her reminiscing on all the things she had learned in my class and about life was quite gospel-like to me during future demanding times.

Trying to keep this book in chronological order is very demanding. I can only hope that you are keeping up. In the school year of 1996–1997, we were once again perched at the top of the high school football world at Cummings High. Wrestling was expected to do well also. I basically recovered from my wreck injuries, my heart was having its moments, but I was functional, pulling twelve- to fourteen-hour days, teaching my classes, and coaching my two sports.

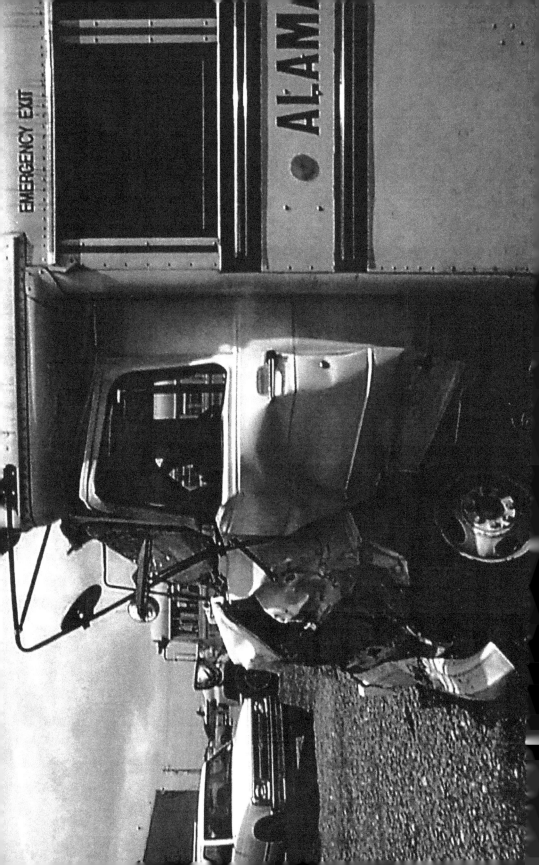

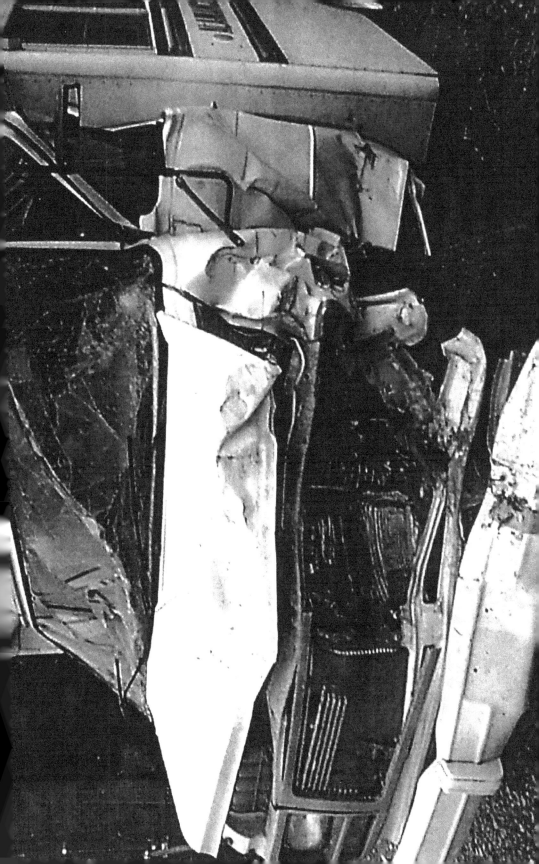

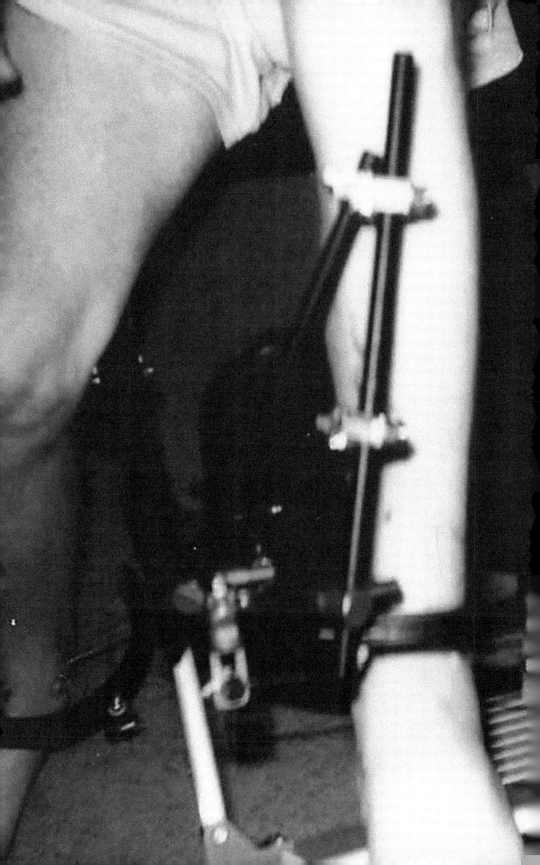

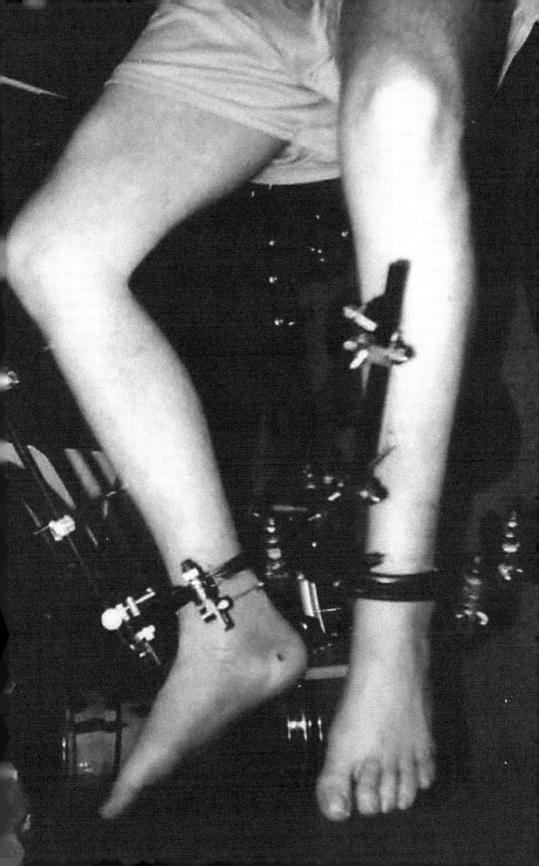

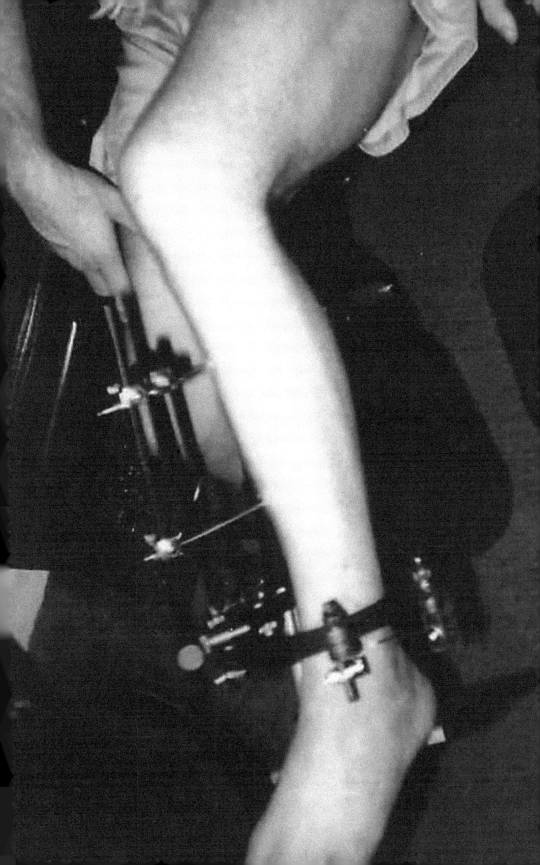

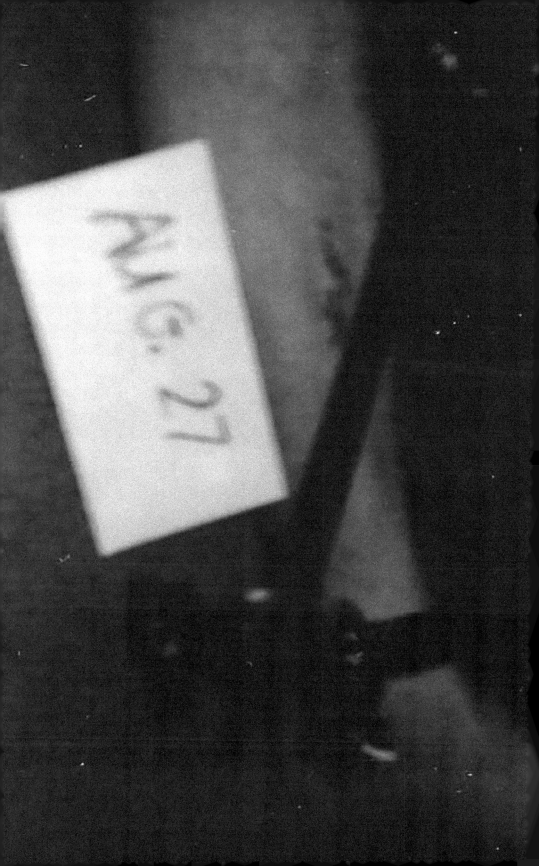

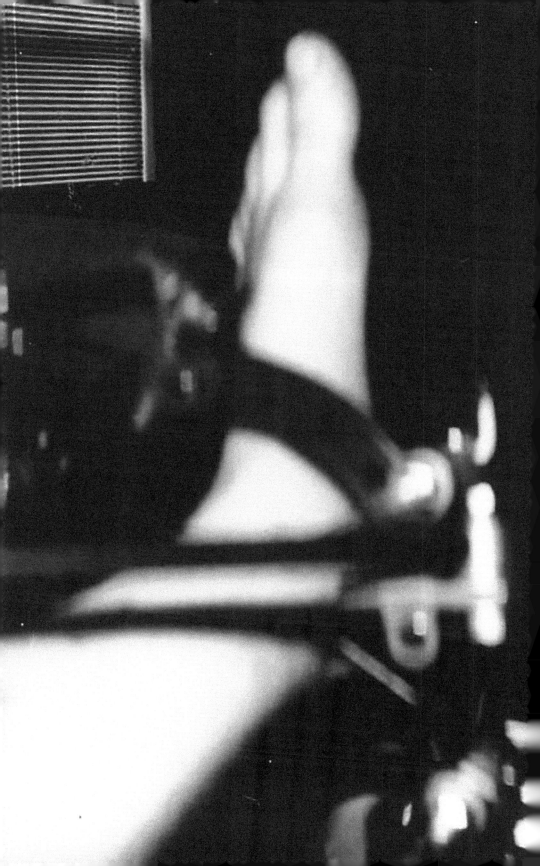

CHAPTER 9

Another Great Moment

In the school year of 1996–1997, we were standing on the sidelines coaching, visiting on of our toughest conference rivals, the Reidsville Rams. We were battling for the top spot in the conference and, probably, the top spot in the state polls as well. My coaching family and I were very busy to say the least. They would score, and we would score, back and forth. This went on for the whole first half. We left the sideline concerned and pondering what adjustments needed to be made and contemplating the second half.

As we made our way to the locker room, a young fellow teacher (I'll call her Sam) approached me and said, "Cheer up, you have just won a truck."

I asked her, "What?" because she was making no sense with that statement, especially with the crowd's noise, so I just kept walking.

After the game and all the excitement with the long ride home, after taking my shower, I proceeded to go straight to bed. I was awakened the next morning (Saturday) with the telephone continually ringing. I finally picked up the phone and said, "Yeah?"

The voice on the other end of the phone asked, "Is this Mr. Hawks?"

I replied that it was, and the voice on the other end said, "Congratulations, you are the 1996–1997 Dickies Work Apparel, American Worker of the Year."

My response was, "What! You must have the wrong number. I haven't entered any contest."

The representative on the other end said, "Your coworker Sam had entered your name in the American Worker of the Year in the United States contest. You have been chosen in recognition of the demanding work, your individual spirit, and sheer perseverance of an American worker. Your work with young people on and off the campus has been recognized by your coworkers and summed up in a contest application and essay written by your coworker Sam."

Sam had included in her essay that I had become a type of surrogate father to this heterogeneously mixed group of young men, my students and athletes. The representative went on to explain on the phone that I had won a brand-new 1997 Chevrolet truck, an unlimited supply of Dickies work apparel, a cash prize, and a chance to appear on the *Good Morning America* show airing from New York and the *Grand Ole Opry* in Nashville, Tennessee.

I was in shock and kept asking the guy on the phone, "Are you sure you have the right guy?"

He replied, "Certainly, I'm sure. We'll call you on Monday and set up a convenient time when we can come in from New York." They would be coming to take some pictures, watch the kids, and possibly do an interview.

I told them that would be great, still in disbelief, as I hung up the phone. The words that Sam had said to me the night before while walking off the field at half-time finally made sense. "Cheer up, you won a truck." I looked up Sam's number in the phone book and gave her a call, inquiring, "What did you do?"

She said, "I entered you in a contest that I felt was truly about you. Someone that is a hard worker to the point of having it rub off on everyone around you, like the kids you teach and coach, and work alongside of. They would walk through fire for you. You have done so much for so many, it's time that someone did something just for you." After all, she just had to tell the truth. I thanked her, but I had no clue as to what else to say.

The following Monday, Dickies Work Apparel had their publicist get in touch with me. I got a call in which I was told they would be sending out a representative and a photographer on the upcoming Friday. I agreed and proceeded through my week. Of course, by the time the week played out, a lot of attention had headed my way but, more importantly, to my school athletes and students. During the week, the principal called me in the office to tell me how proud she was of my efforts.

She said, "Hawks, most teachers need a break from the kids on the weekends and afternoons. However, on the other hand, you spend your downtime with them. This is beyond the call of duty, and we are very proud of you."

I told her, "Every teacher is the American Worker of the Year, if the public ever stood up and noticed what we did for a living."

Some think they understand, but not really. So the week went on with all the local newspapers, television stations, radio stations covering this event. I felt very humbled and honored. It was unique to be honored for doing stuff that I had been doing all my life, which just seemed to be the right stuff. Isn't that what we're all supposed to do, the right thing? I remembered my grandfather telling me, "You can only do the best you can do. You may not succeed, but all you can do is the best that you can do."

I sat back one day to reflect on all this attention coming my way, and I know I'm not supposed to, but I began to do the glass-half-empty-or-half-full thing. I wasn't basking in the limelight because I had just done what I had all my life. I had always had some kind of complex about not letting anyone down, especially if they were counting on me. This huge cloud of responsibility hangs over me to this day. I will even disappoint myself if I can't live up to the expectations others have of me. I know you're getting ready to say the book's title again, "Coach, are you crazy?"

Well, maybe you are thinking about all I have been through to this point. You remember the heart problem, then the wreck, now the accolades, but I had begun to remember some unpleasantries that went along with the deal.

What am I specifically referring to? I suddenly remembered returning to the hospital after my rehabilitation period was over to get the halos and rods taken off and removed from the insides of my legs. You know, after the wreck. I remembered the doctor entering the room and saying, "This will only take a moment, relax." He then took out a common drill and proceeded to put a socket on the end of it. I'm sitting there in amazement as he placed the socket on the end of the rods and screwed into the shinbone of both my lower legs; he then placed the drill into reverse and drilled the rods out.

The first rod came out quickly with the hole smoking on the surface of my legs, and blood spattered moderately. The pain was excruciating. I yelled, "Hey, doc, aren't you going to numb it?"

He said, "This will only take a minute."

I grabbed the pillow from the examination table and began to bite down on it. What seemed to be an eternity probably happened pretty quickly. But, hey, when's the last time you saw four holes in your legs with smoke coming out of them? I breathed heavily for a moment while the doctor gave me and the drill a rest. I couldn't help but think about a joke I used to tell the kids as I grasped that pillow for dear life. A man had a dream that he had swallowed the world's biggest marshmallow. He woke up the next morning, and his pillow was gone.

Before I could grin from my own silliness, here comes the doctor again asking me if I was ready to continue. He had what looked like a pair of needle-nose pliers that were going to pull out the wires that were still in my lower legs. The wires were crossing inside my ankles and protruding from the outside from four opposing angles. The doctor, with help from an assistant holding my legs, grabbed the ends of those protruding wires to pull them out, much to my amazement and displeasure.

As he continued to pull on these embedded wires about the thickness of a coat hanger, I began to hear the bones pop and crackle. Guess what? It seemed endless with the pop and crackle and more excruciating pain and even more blood. As I continued to chew and grasp on my newest friend, the pillow, I suddenly gasped a sigh of relief. It was finally over.

After a few minutes, I was fitted with a new set of crutches to replace my wheelchair. I guess you are now beginning to understand I have accomplished some pretty amazing things in my sixty-three years on this earth. But I have paid a terrible price for success. Especially in some instances, to quote the doctor who treated me after the wreck. He said, "No matter how much money they offer you in a settlement for this wreck, they can't pay you enough for what they've done to you." The wreck wasn't my fault; the other driver got the ticket, but that wouldn't fix what I had gone through and what awaited me in the future. They can call you a hero, but the reality was going to set in soon with these stiff legs.

So the television folks from the area and the publicists from Dickies showed up on Friday with lengthy interviews and photographs of the story of how a country boy who was a teacher and coach had become the American Worker of the Year in the United States. On their first visit, the Dickies publicist took pictures of the kids who helped make this award possible. Loading and unloading wood, mowing grass, etc. The next visit was in the upcoming weekend when they visited football practice and actually stood on the sidelines during the game. It seemed different coaching with cameras watching your every move and large disklike microphones picking up every sound on the sidelines. It was a wonderful experience for the kids, who liked to ham it up on the sidelines in front of the camera crews.

My next adventure would be the following weekend when I would fly to New York City to be on the *Good Morning America* show. I had interviews set up with Charlie Gaddy and Susan Vargas. The flight was short, and dawn came early, around 4:30 AM, to prepare for the television cameras.

I had been on television many times before, but I didn't know what I was in for. A limousine picked me up in front of the hotel a little before 5:00 AM, and the day began. I was whisked away to a television station makeup room where they proceeded to pancake down my face, eyebrows, and all. When I finally looked in the mirror, I looked orange. I had packed a fancy suit and tie for the affair hoping to look my best. Thank God, I had packed my usual casual-guy wardrobe. Upon arrival at the hotel the night before, the representatives from Dickies informed me that they wanted me dressed in their attire: khakis, blue shirt with the Dickies logo on it, and a pair of Dickies work boots.

A lot of people would probably have had a little stage fright somewhere along the way, but I've been on TV before, interviewed before, and had been to New York several times, so for me, the shock wasn't bad at all. The night before the show, I went out on the town with the Dickies representatives for dinner. We also took in some of the sights as well. New York City is an amazing place. It's kind of like Las Vegas, a city that never sleeps and has something going on all night long.

It's kinda like the people who live there don't want to waste one precious moment of life. I love to visit the big cities, but this country boy loves coming home. After about a week among the skyscrapers and all those people, I would be climbing the walls. A weekend like I was experiencing, however, was exhilarating.

For someone like me who's used to going out into the front yard and seeing maybe one house for about a mile around, living in a high-rise looking down on people scurrying like ants on the ground below seems difficult to understand. Just like my situation, I guess if that's all you've ever known, that would be the norm.

Talking with some of the native New Yorkers was fun. They thought I could possibly be from another country with what they described as a thick Southern accent. I thought their dialect was funny as well. So we spent a lot of time just talking. On my final night, I went for a walk, and it's even hard to imagine when you step out on a main street at night. You have to stay to the right to prevent from getting swept away like an ant going the wrong direction up an anthill.

I flagged down a cab and immediately jumped inside. My being from the country and probably more talkative than most Yankees are used to, I began to try and strike up a conversation with the driver. He was simply unresponsive; he never said a word. Taking a chance on making him mad, I said, "What's the matter with you? Did the Jets lose or something?"

He peered up in the rearview mirror with a steely look and said, "Jesus Christ, a Jethro Bodine comedian."

We both burst out laughing, and a conversation ensued. As we pulled up in front of my hotel, I got out and asked him how much I owed him.

He replied, "Are you in a hurry?" and I said, "No, I got all night."

He put down the flag and said, "Get in."

I hopped into the front seat of the cab, and he took me on a real tour of New York City, narrating all the sights like a tour guide.

I told him I had noticed all the cab drivers I had encountered since being in New York seemed to be Arabic.

He replied humorously, "Yeah, they are all camel jockeys but me."

We spent most of the night just riding around and seeing the city. Just before the sun came up, I arrived back at my hotel. As I got out, I asked, "What do I owe you?" and he responded, "Take care of yourself, country boy, and stay crazy."

I replied, "I'll do that. You take care of yourself."

With that, he spun away. Entering the lobby, I realized I had made another friend, probably whom I would never see again, but that was irrelevant.

I guess you are wondering what happened on TV. The morning just passed away. After all the makeup, I had to go to wardrobe to make sure I had all the Dickies clothing on and had that all-American worker look, if you know what I mean. After sitting in a waiting room for quite a while, a GMA producer came in. She laid out the procedure for the show in which I'd be involved and a copy of the questions to be asked in the interview. After each one of her instructions, she kept saying, "Now, don't be nervous." She then left me alone to ponder the upcoming event.

I was reading over the questions, planning out my responses, and all the while, I kept hearing her say, "Don't be nervous." Guess what? I began to get nervous, but the longer I rehearsed, the more comfortable I got as the big moment neared. They took me to a place behind the stage curtain. I could hear the show in progress, and the female producer stood beside me and instructed me which chair to sit in and what camera to face.

I'm thinking all the while, *I sure hope I remember all of this.* A commercial break came, and then I heard the host, Charlie Gaddy, introduce me as I walked on to the stage and took a seat. It was surprisingly comfortable. After all, I was about to do what I do best: *talk.* The lights were ungodly bright and scorching hot. Now I know why they had used so much makeup. Because if you didn't use the makeup, your face would shine on camera.

The interview by Charlie Gaddy lasted about fifteen minutes, and then came another commercial break. I left the stage while one more guest performed at the very end of the show. She had invented some new type of dishes that she presented on the show in buffet form. We would all pig out after the show, and I would get to talk with Charlie Gaddy and Susan Vargas. I told Susan Vargas that she should go out with my roommate. He had a crush on her. She told me she would, but she was currently dating Lyle Lovett. My response with a frowned face was, "Why?" We both burst out laughing.

After my exciting cab ride from the night before, I would arise the next day to say goodbye for now to New York and catch a flight home.

People called all that weekend to tell me that they saw the interview and how well it had gone. On the following Monday, my coworkers responded in the same complimentary fashion, so I guess I didn't bomb, as they say in showbiz.

A lot of publicity soon followed, some local TV and a lot of newspaper articles, and, yes, I got to model some clothes in the Dickies catalog. A local television station was running a series at the time titled, *What's Right with Our Schools?* My award interview and the kids were involved on air with a video of me teaching in class, coaching during a football game, and splitting and cutting wood with the kids.

I received phone calls from our then-superintendent and many other school and county officials for which I still feel honored to this day. Meanwhile, the accolades started to roll in, and so did the clothes. In one of our first meetings, the Dickies folks had asked my sizes in just about everything, from gloves, boots, shirts, T-shirts, hats, caps, jeans, and so forth. A large box arrived one a week on my front door with not only all types of clothes but all sizes. I began to look forward to my weekly Dickies "Christmas" package.

I had so many clothes in so many sizes that I began to first hand them to the kids who worked for me, and my friends and neighbors. Dickies for everybody. Meanwhile, the local newspaper continued to print articles like "Local Teacher/Coach Continues to Help Students After Award." I was very honored and thrilled.

Meanwhile, Dickies of Fort Worth, Texas, was planning some even bigger events. The next would be a trip to Nashville, Tennessee, to appear on the *Grand Ole Opry*. There I would receive a plaque designating me as the American Worker of the Year and a certificate for a brand-new Chevrolet pickup truck, and some cash. Not bad, huh? They informed me that I could bring a guest, so I decided to bring Sam. After all, she was partly responsible for this anyway. You remember Sam, my coworker who had nominated me for the award.

They gave Sam a speaking role in the award presentation, so she got to be on TV as well. It was a way of saying thanks. So two weekends later, on to Nashville for us. Some way or another, this trip seemed longer. There was more time to sightsee and dine and even some time to relax. I was still teaching, coaching, and flying to Tennessee for the weekend, being on the *Grand Ole Opry* live, and being in front of my class back on Monday morning. It was pretty stressful. But what the heck, I was young then.

Sam and I spent the night before the broadcast dining with the dignitaries of Dickies and the *Grand Ole Opry*. There we would hear how to commercialize the contest winner's future exposures, etc. What would happen the next afternoon during the awards presentation was discussed. Then we all went on a sightseeing tour before returning to the hotel.

The next day arrived with me just walking around the hotel. The Opryland hotel in Nashville was huge. I had never seen anything so big in my life, not even in New York City, Las Vegas, or Atlantic City. Don't get me wrong. All those aforementioned places have their own special ambiance unto themselves, but the place was huge. It reminded me of a super indoor shopping mall with five to six stories or levels, with doors right along the walkways that led into the hotel rooms. It also had beautiful giant fountains, waterfalls, and peacocks walking around. The Opryland Hotel was kind of like a museum, mall, and hotel all covering a vast amount of acreage.

The day came for the awards ceremony. We were informed that it would occur as a live presentation onstage during the weekly Saturday night performance, televised in front of a live audience. This time, as before, I had packed another one of my fancy suits and ties, and I would be able to wear it on stage this time. Upon arrival, they introduced us to Porter Wagoner, the long-time host of the *Grand Ole Opry*, a country music star in his own right. It was a real treat, especially finding him to be a nice, down-to-earth regular guy.

My grandparents and I used to watch him and Dolly Parton on a black-and-white TV, so this was very special to me. Sam had rehearsed her part to a tee and didn't seem nervous at all. All of a sudden, girls started screaming backstage as some young, tall, and good-looking country singer entered the backstage door, cowboy hat in place, clinging to a giant guitar case. I looked at Sam, trying to understand what all the commotion was about. She leaned over and whispered the name of some up-and-coming country star. I don't even remember his name.

Don't get me wrong. I'm just not a big country music fan. But I enjoy all music, country as well. I like any of the arts, including music, but that being said, it was pretty amazing to be behind the scenes, especially while the show was in progress.

Suddenly the show began with Porter Wagoner going out to introduce the first act. When they began to play the music, Porter, Jan, the Dickies rep, the producer, Sam, and I met momentarily behind the stage curtain to get a last-minute overview of what was going to happen, how it would play out.

After the next song was over, Porter Wagoner would go out and introduce Sam and me. We would then enter the stage taking a place at two microphones, which were numbered. After Porter was finished, Sam would read the letter she had written to Dickies and why she had nominated me. Then a representative from Dickies would appear from behind the curtain to say a few words.

I would then receive the award and make a short speech. Porter Wagoner said something, and Sam and I would exit the stage. When we were finished, there was tremendous applause. Once we wiped off the sweat, we began to laugh and relax, hanging out backstage, talking and laughing with some of the performers.

When we all met behind the curtain, I remember seeing Porter Wagoner chain-smoking one cigarette after another as he peered through a slit in the curtain.

I asked, "Are you nervous?"

He replied, "Oh, man, I have been doing this show for years, and I get just as nervous now as I did the first time I ever walked out there."

I replied, "Dang, maybe I should have been nervous," to which everyone laughed.

That was a fond memory because Porter Wagoner would die a few years later. At the mention of his death, I remembered him and our conversation. We hung out for hours behind the scenes backstage at the *Grand Ole Opry*, listening to the music and taking in all the activity.

Later on, in the evening, everyone met again for a meal. I would discuss with the Dickies representative about future obligations as well. But hey, up till now, I was going home with a plaque, a certificate to purchase a new pickup for $27,000 and some cash, not to mention my new stash of Dickies apparel. It was a special time, one I would never forget.

I still reminisce about what it took and what I have been through to get here. All those fourteen-hour workdays, the heart trouble, and that hellacious wreck. I had quite a coaching record by now and then this award. I guess everything's a trade-off in life.

The next day, Sam and I walked around the Opryland Hotel taking a last look and shopping for souvenirs. People would approach us saying things like, "Hey, we saw you last night on the *Grand Ole Opry*. Could we have your autograph?"

Of course, we talked with all those curious folks, signed a few autographs, and gathered stuff to head to the airport, saying goodbye to Tennessee for now, with a long flight home lying ahead. I got home at 1:00 AM. I'm glad I was young then.

I returned to work on Monday with many coworkers wishing me well. The kids talked about the show and my mentioning them and the school on TV. My response was, "We're all in this together." As I said, when accepting that award in Nashville, it represented the challenging work of every teacher and student at Cummings High School. So from all of them and myself, thank you.

Now, most people would say, "What a life you've led." Well, hang in there till you hear what's ahead. I bet you're asking somewhere along about now, What about the heart problem? Well, don't get me wrong. I could definitely tell something was wrong, some days more than others. But I was functional. My six-month visits to my heart specialist showed me how lucky I was. After all, he expressed how all those long days would be challenging for someone with no health problems to deal with, much less someone with them.

He still constantly expressed to me how amazing it was for me to get done what I had done. I've told him each time we talk, I realize how fortunate I am, and that I'm making the most of every day I have on this earth, to make it a better place and enjoy the opportunities with which I've been blessed.

We won some conference championships in wrestling and football, but the next big events would come in 2001, both for the school, the teams I helped, and for me personally as well.

Oh, I know you would want to hear this. Remember the American Worker of the Year contest? Well, it went on after my winning for a few years, then was discontinued. Rocky Boots out of Ohio purchased Dickies Work Apparel and abruptly discontinued the "lifetime" of clothing. Then, after a few years, they started the contest again. First prize was a million dollars. Can you believe that? I started to ask them if I could reenter—no, I'm just kidding, but can you believe it? It was a wonderful ride.

The memories made getting there, the lives that were changed along the way, and the relationships forged were precious to me. Those were all just as valuable to me as the truck, plaque, and everything else.

Funny story about the truck. I received a coupon so that I could redeem it at a local Chevrolet dealership in my area. I'm a Ford guy, so shopping for a Chevrolet seemed highly out of character. After many visits to all the local dealerships, I found a model that would best suit my needs. It was a large four-door and powerful. It was a type of work truck, but to me, it was beautiful. I know it was a Chevrolet, but it represented all that arduous work by those kids and me over the years and a trophy of sorts for surviving all those tragedies. I picked up my truck just in time for my birthday. I was forty-something by now, and little did I know I was about to fall victim to a midlife crisis. I built a garage for my new truck and only drove it on special occasions.

After all, I already had two old work trucks. One was the Mule, my old Ford F-150, and a part of the Hawks's family. I also had a 1982 Chevrolet Dually. Both of them were pretty beat-up, and after all, if we used the new truck in the tree business, within a couple of years, it would look like the other two.

So under the garage, the home made especially for it, she sat. All new and shiny and white. She was a reminder as a prize for all those years of demanding work by so many. Then one day, while working in the yard, a young guy stopped by in a brand-new Mustang convertible. He expressed his desire to trade this wonderful ride he owned for my new truck. I hadn't thought about trading or selling my newly acquired trophy. But for the sake of consideration, we went for a ride in his new convertible, with me, naturally, at the wheel.

We drove around Graham with the top down. This sleek, powerful open-air machine was awesome. Okay, I was having a flashback. My midlife crisis was showing. At least I hadn't had a hair transplant. When we arrived back at my house, we started the horse-trading process. I told him I'd swap him, and he'd give me $10,000 to boot. His reply was, "Hell, no." But I began to explain to him that both his car and my truck were the same year and relatively had the same amount of mileage, and a truck was worth more on the open market. His reply was the same as before. He drove away still wanting a new Chevrolet truck, and I stood on my deck knowing for one of the few times in my life I had fallen in love. Well, he drove out of sight, and I went back to working on whatever it was I had been working on, trying to put that beautiful black Mustang convertible out of my mind.

After a couple of days and thoughts of my many other responsibilities had taken over, the young man drove up into my yard once again, with the top down and music blaring. I walked up to him, and he said while sitting in my new truck, "Let's do it." I went in the house and got the title to my trophy. We then proceeded to the bank to do the necessary transfers. When we returned to my house, I watched as my truck went down the road. Then I looked in the garage at my newly acquired prize, which I still own today. Yep, it's sitting in the garage with about 18,000 miles on it. Not bad for a twenty-one-year-old beauty. It now represents all the challenging work of those kids and myself. Okay, it also serves as a symbol of my midlife crisis. Who cares? It's beautiful and fun to drive.

We continued our winning ways in athletics at Cummings. In 2007, we had an exceptional football team and won three championships on the way to the state championship at Kenan Stadium at the University of North Carolina campus in Chapel Hill.

We came into the game against an opponent we would have many a fracas with over the next several years. They'd beat us, and we would beat them and always in the same state championship. They would switch coaches over the next several years, but their tenacity and athleticism would not change. I'm speaking of the Sampson County powerhouse, Clinton High School.

We came into the game with one of the most prolific passing games in the state. It would be plotted against future NFL start Willie Parker, who would play for the University of North Carolina at Chapel Hill and then for the Pittsburg Steelers. To say they had a running attack along with those other bruisers they had in the backfield was an understatement.

It was a beautiful day. The field was set. Kenan Stadium was packed, and it's going to be the run versus the pass. So let's get started. The game was everything we had thought it was going to be. They'd score, we'd score, with only a few points separating us at any given moment. As for Willie Parker, we'd never find any answer for him. Our own defense had played well all year and continued throughout this game. But as the game wound on with that punishing, bruising, running, and having to tackle those big running backs time after time, these began to wear us down. To our credit, however, they never found an answer to our passing attack either.

Only problem was we'd score very quickly, like lightning on their secondary, and then we would kick off to them. They would start one of those long seven-minute drives eating up the clock. This was their best defense against the passing game. Keeping the ball out of our hands. There was very little difference in the score at halftime. But it was a grueling contest, and as we migrated to the locker room, you could see the story of the game on both opponents' faces.

The second half would prove to be a carbon copy of the first half until one big play. Late in the game, with only a small deficit and Clinton driving, one of our starting secondary players came up lame with a cramp. We had to substitute a younger less-experienced player in his place.

On the third down, they threw a pass in the area of our substitute who grabbed the Clinton receiver but was dragged off on his way to the goal line. He scored. That deficit would be too much for the Cummings Cavaliers to overcome. So as time expired, we had finished second in the state championship. Not bad, hey? A spot millions of teams wished they could be in. Not us, however. We knew if not for one play, we had let it get away from us.

An unquenchable thirst hung on our lips as we left the football field that day. In the locker room, we knew we had many returnees coming back. Many of us made up our minds right then and there, especially the kids, that we were going to return.

Once again, wrestling was successful, having a winning record and many tournaments. Lots of kids enjoyed successes that year. Then, after a very long wrestling season, it was over. I mean when you go to the state championship in football, you have played sixteen games. I started wrestling in late July and finished right before Christmas. Wrestling had already begun, so I was coaching both at the same time. If we went to the state championship in wrestling as we always did, I am talking about ending my year of coaching in late February. By now, I was bone tired. I know you're asking yourself the title of the book again, Coach, are you crazy?

This year was no different from others. We were used to having success at Cummings, and why not? We had outstanding athletes, superior coaches, and support from the school and the community. There was nothing missing. Steve Johnson was once asked by a reporter about his football staff. He replied, "Any one of them could be a successful head coach any time they wished." He has called all of us one of the finest coaching staffs in the state, of which many agree.

Especially me. I am a true believer. Although we disagree occasionally on strategy, we're all team players and think of each other as brothers and family members. We want what's best for the kids and their success. All of us respect each other and one another's knowledge of the game. Each one of us brings something special to the table, and it's an important part of the mix. I will call it success.

March 2001 rolled around, and my friend, the athletic director football coach Jay Perdue called me into the athletic office and said, "Congratulations."

I asked, "On what?"

He replied, "You're going to be pictured in the North Carolina Wall of Fame as one of North Carolina's greatest coaches. Your picture will be displayed on the wall in Chapel Hill, at the North Carolina High School Athletic Association offices."

A few days later, I received my letter of acknowledgement based on records and a picture that now sits in Chapel Hill. To date, this is one of my highest honors. I coached all the guys that I had the opportunity to and was able to share in their successes. I want to say to all those people, "Thanks to all of you. You are each part of that success in Chapel Hill."

Many times, things start happening so fast in your life, you don't really have time to absorb just what's happened until much later. During times of reflection, I take pride in all the honors that have been bestowed upon me. As for the terrible things, a coach once told me, "Whatever tragedies in your life that don't kill you just make you stronger." I don't know if I'd go far enough to buy into that or not, but maybe, you'll be a better judge of that than me by the time we get to the end of this book. When reflecting on the Wall of Fame, it never really hit me until a visit to the wall one day, seeing all those honorable colleagues there on the shelf with me; it made it really sink in.

The athletic year of 2002 would roll around next. You've heard of a roller-coaster ride? Then, you pay attention to this. During the summer, while all my friends and I sat in the Cummings's head coach's office, planning the year's upcoming football practices, a familiar face appeared. A local star on one of the football teams from a neighboring county appeared in our office, stating that he had transferred to Cummings. We all looked at each other, and the head coach informed him that he couldn't go to Cummings if he didn't live in our school zone. If we had talked with him before he was officially enrolled, it could be considered recruiting. He informed us that he had already enrolled and had been cleared through our local county offices. We then, not trying to be counterproductive, informed the young man he'd have to be living with his legal guardian in our school zone to be eligible. He assured us he was all the above. When asked why he and his family had moved, he said he didn't know why; they just had. We informed him he'd have to give us several days to check out the situation more thoroughly, with which he seemed perfectly satisfied. After a week or so, a call from our local county offices had cleared him to play. This guy had played in our conference as our opponent for several years.

We already knew him to be an outstanding athlete in football and was a state champion in one of the sprinting events in track. Very seldom do you get this type of gift as a coach. But we accepted it as a piece of good luck, one of the few that we had that year.

The 2002 football started with a bang, with our mighty Cavaliers looking to avenge last year's loss in the state championship. After all, we had the nucleus of last year's state runners-up back. We were big, quick, athletic, and hungry. We still had that unquenched thirst and that empty feeling of losing the state championship game the previous year. It was probably the biggest game we'd all coached together up to this point.

We started the year by reeling off six straight victories, sitting atop the 2-A polls in the state of North Carolina, along with our next opponent, the Reidsville Rams. The table was set for a big game. Now it's not just my imagination, but it seemed like the upcoming years when we didn't win the state championship in football, Reidsville did and vice versa. To put a little more icing on the cake, we were in the same conference for several years. To make it even more interesting, the state came out with a new criterion, dividing 2-A and 3-A classifications into 2-A and 2-AA, 3-A and 3-AA, according to enrollment size in those classifications.

So game number 7 was here. Both undefeated teams were sitting atop the state standings and conferences as well. Both had premier athletes, stingy defenses, and experienced coaches. In other words, they were probably the two most evenly matched teams in the state. The game was in Reidsville, however, which we figured was good for a touchdown or less difference.

Friday arrived with great anticipation. Little did we know what lay ahead. After school, we met at the pregame meal, a ritual for years. Once we returned, we began handing out the pants and the game jerseys for that night's game. The principal came down to the cage where we kept all the equipment and said that she needed to speak with the head coach.

After a short behind-closed-doors session, she left the coach with a disgusted look on his face. Coach Johnson stated that we couldn't use our premier running back in the game that night. You remember, the one who had transferred in from a neighboring high school.

There seemed to be some questions still about his eligibility that were unanswered. We were all in shock. I mean, he had been cleared by our local school system's central office. What else could we do? Since our principal had just informed us not to use this winning running back until we got this problem solved, we had little choice.

We had to inform the young man in question; he couldn't dress out until we found a solution. What a helpless feeling; there was nothing we could do now. I will always remember that disappointed face; after all, it wasn't his fault, or ours either. We had done everything in our power, by the book, but nevertheless, we were in a mess.

We took our traveling show over to Reidsville, one man less. It was a terrific game, but at the end, we came up short. Would our starting running back have made a difference? Well, I'm not sure, but I would have felt better with him in there.

The first loss of the season had been hung on us, and all those bitter feelings of losing the state championship the year before came rushing back. Plus, now there was a new wrinkle. Until now, we had been undefeated. Now our state championship hope had been dealt its first taste of doubt. After all, we just knew we would see Reidsville again in the playoffs.

The big question was, Would our best running back be the difference next time? There wasn't a lot of time for second-guessing. We would have to regroup and start over on Monday. During that part of the school year,

I had fourth period free because I coached two sports. This arrangement would make class preparations easier; getting buses and preparing for practices and right-after-school events could be seen to as well.

Upon entering the coaching office, I was informed that the High School Athletics Association was meeting about the situation on our transferred running back and would give us an answer at the beginning of the week as to what they thought. The next day would bring an unwelcomed answer. The powers-that-be had ruled our running back was eligible for the rest of the season, but in the best interest of all concerned, we would have to forfeit all the six games we had won.

It was a question of who had custody of him, and was he living with that person? Our question was, well, if he's eligible now, why wasn't he eligible then? He hadn't moved since he had originally come to play with us. Someone was getting appeased somewhere. It was too late to worry about that now. We started off 6 and 0, and now we were 0 and 7 with having lost only one game on the field.

We also had the unenviable task of telling our kids that they were now 0 and 6 after being undefeated. They took it as any young aspiring group would. Disappointed looks, heads down. But many of them, after being informed we'd have to win the rest of the way to make the playoffs, found themselves filled with a new resolve.

Some of them were even yelling as we broke into groups for practice that day, "We can do it, we'll show them!" Guess what? They were right.

Now comes another bad twist in the story. During the year, we had played some of the toughest opponents in the state, Dudley, Thomasville, and of course, our good friends, the Reidsville Rams. A weariness with all the ups and downs of this season was starting to show on all of us. Our head coach Steve Johnson collapsed and was diagnosed with Guillain-Barré syndrome, which left him unable to walk. He was very sick for a long time.

Of course, we were all very worried. Our leader's health was more important than all the adversity we were going through on all other fronts. We sat in a meeting just looking at one another, and I said, "Dang, what else?" With worrying about our leader and all the other things happening around us, we all rolled up our sleeves and got down to business. We pulled a Rocky Balboa with comeback number 68 (the great comeback).

Now comes the part of life you should never do any-way, but we all caught ourselves doing it. You know, when asking yourself why was all this serious stuff happening to us, or me personally? After all, these men I work with are some of the finest on earth. I can truly speak to that cause. Remember, I've worked everywhere. These guys are truly about whatever it takes for the kids. That's what they are all about.

These kids had worked so hard. They did everything they had been asked to do. Entering this season with their "eyes on the prize," the state championship, and suddenly, we asked, Where were all these obstacles coming from? They would not be denied, and to their credit, they regrouped, and with seven losses under their belts, they proceeded to finish the rest of the season with four straight wins. We had made it into the playoffs despite all that had happened.

Coach Jay Perdue had assumed the head coaching position duties in our head coach's absence, a very rigorous job. Having to answer all the questions about forfeiting all those games in the beginning of the season was very difficult. After all, we had done nothing wrong but still found ourselves in a rather untenable position.

We were all supportive and tried to shoulder some of the load, but to quote the familiar phrases about leadership, "It's lonely at the top," and "This might be the only election in history where the winner demands a recount." So there, we went into the playoffs, with a losing record for the first time since I had been there. We had finished second in the conference.

Our first game would take us to the mountains to play perennial power Newton Conover, undefeated and unscored on in many quarters. Our kids rose to the occasion, first jumping on their powerful opponent, scoring in the high forties on the scoreboard and dominating every phase of the game.

A funny moment occurred as we passed through the line, shaking hands with the opposing players and coaches. One of their giant offensive lineman yelled out, "Four and 7, who the hell have you been playing, the San Francisco 49ers?" to which we all laughed. We knew their disappointment, for we had been there ourselves. Not to worry though, they would win themselves a state championship too. As a matter of fact, it was only two years later.

We would reel off victories the rest of the way until we were there again. This time it was in Winston-Salem at Wake Forest University home field for the state championship. Guess who the opponent was? Yeah, you guessed it, our other old buddies, the Clinton Dark Horses who had defeated us in Chapel Hill for the state championship. Many had graduated from both teams, but there were still some remaining.

The battle was on. Prior to the game, Coach Steve Johnson entered the locker room in a wheelchair to cheers. He would stand, and as he talked to our players, he produced a newspaper of the state championship from the year before. It read, CLINTON DEFEATS CUMMINGS IN THE STATE CHAMPIONSHIP. This brought back those haunting feelings of what it was like to watch that clock tick down while you were behind, knowing your dreams had come up short. He pretty much resurrected those old memories and told them, "Don't let that happen again."

We went out and took the field as our leader was being pushed in a wheelchair. He was still unable to stand on the sidelines, but he was in the front row of the bleachers in the stands, within shouting distance in case we needed some instructions.

Once we were on the field, a few hecklers began yelling obscenities at our coaches. From what I could gather, they were blaming us for all the difficulties we had encountered up to this point in the season. I was thinking to myself as Coach Foust and several others became angry. *What is the matter with those people?* Now, mind you, it was only a handful, but they didn't have a clue of what it took to get here, especially with what those kids and we coaches had been through.

I mean, man, it was close to a miracle status. The game was hard hitting. We went down and scored on our first drive. Then we kicked off to them after the extra point. They had set up the wall we had worked against all week right down our sidelines, got their running back behind it, and ran it all the way back for a touchdown.

Here we are looking at ourselves and thinking, *Here we go again*. The rest of the game remained a strong, well-coached affair with no team able to open up more than a touchdown lead. It was a typical Clinton Dark Horse game. They were big and aggressive but so were we. We had our running game clicking on all cylinders to go with our legendary passing attack. The game played out with the Clinton Dark Horses clinging to a touchdown and an extra point to lead late in the fourth quarter, and the ball was on their own twenty-seven-yard line.

On fourth and inches, their coaching staff made a fatal error. Instead of punting the ball and putting us deep on our end of the field, they chose to go for it. See, their strategy was they would go for it on the fourth down, and if they made it, they would run the clock out even if they just stayed in the huddle. However, if you decide to go for it, you had better make it. It's kind of like those religious bumper stickers on cars, "If you're living like there's no God, you had better be right."

The Dark Horses lined up in regular formation, and we were yelling instructions for our kids we had deep, to move up due to their going for it. Our defensive coordinator, Coach Frank Mensch, called a stunt or blitz off the corner, and we got an unbelievable push up the middle. Their talented quarterback was tackled for a loss, and our defense ran off the field in celebration.

We had new life, but very little precious time remained. We all agreed the play calling on offense would become very aggressive, and on the third down, what we would later call the catch would be made by one of our receivers in the back of the end zone. He would go up in a crowd and come down with the ball. The extra point was good.

We had a tied ball game. After a series by Clinton and not to make the same mistake twice, we wound up with the ball after three plays, being right in front of the uprights. Our kicker kicked a twenty-something-yard field goal. While it was on its way, before it had even reached the uprights, he began to run off the field, hands held in the air, signaling it was good.

He knew before any of us knew, even the officials, before he reached the sideline, it was good, and our kicker was right. We had taken a three-point lead, but it was not over yet. We'd still have to kick off to them, and remember, they had already run one back and scored. Now don't get too tense. Would it happen again? We kicked to them, covered it well, they got tackled, and the clock ran out. The kids began to celebrate.

Tears ran down my face as I looked up at the sky while walking across that field to shake hands with the opposing team. All I could think was, *Thank you, God, thank you.* As I saw the faces of my fellow coaches and our players, I could tell they felt the same way as I did. Looking into the faces of our opponents, I could see the disgust, anger, and disappointment we had felt only a year ago. They were beginning to realize, as we had a year before, they had let one get away.

Unfortunately, that's the way it is in coaching, especially when two great teams meet as we just had. One mistake or decision can be a difference in the outcome. If anyone ever wonders why coaches or players get so nervous before a game, it's not the fear of playing in front of people, it's that fear of the unknown. A break, mistake, or heroism by an athlete that you can't control. A call by the official, good or bad, that turns the game around. I guess many would call it the human element, but it all boils down to that fear of the unknown. We all have it whether we want to admit it or not.

The Clinton coach received so much criticism from the community, he resigned and picked up and moved somewhere else. People were calling him at home and leaving anonymous threatening phone calls. Some were even directed at his children. So much for sportsmanship. It's a shame that after all the support that the teams in a close-knit community like that receives 99 percent of it as positive, but it is shameful that some of the few lose sight of what high school athletics are all about.

Yep, I'm afraid so every community has them. Like the ones that were cursing us as we entered the field to play this remarkable game. It was only three or four, but that's too many. To quote a great coach, "We didn't lose, time just ran out." The Clinton Dark Horses sure have the right to feel that way. But for now, it was our day. After a year, nobody would believe we'd done what looked like the impossible. Headlines in all the newspapers throughout the state read, A COMEBACK FOR THE AGES, and HISTORY DOESN'T REPEAT ITSELF IN WINSTON-SALEM. Also, A FITTING ENDING and RARE BREED, a title I feel that could be used to describe every coach and player on our team.

Coach Steve Johnson said it pretty well when he told us, "The game pretty much emulated our season." All year long we had fought off adversity, and there we were in the fourth quarter fighting it again. It would take weeks for reality to set in, to reflect and look back and really let what we had accomplished sink in.

I'm not just talking about all the stuff that had happened on the road to get there. Mrs. Janie Brown, who had taught all of us coaches at Elon, sent the following letter:

> Dear Coaches Steve, Frank, Jay, Eddie and Andy,
>
> I wanted to send you a hearty congratulation to you all, for your successful football season. I followed the ups and downs of the season with interest, and because I know that you are good guys and I knew that you would survive.
>
> I am quite proud of you. You all must realize that I kind of claim you as

"My boys," since I taught you all. I also assure you that if Coach Brown were living, he too would be proud of you.

Keep up the good work as good professionals. Your good influence reaches many young men. I wish you all the best of both professionally and personally.

God Bless you all,
Janie Brown

With what we overcame to win that state championship, it made our entire coaching staff as close as they could possibly be. As close as the family we had all said we were. These kids would share a special pride and bond that they would carry for the rest of their lives.

The future was bright. Our JV program with myself as head coach had won four or five straight conference championships. These guys began to appear on varsity team, and coupled with the returnees from the miracle season we had just completed, the future was very exciting.

The only sad thing about winning a state championship or winning at anything on a regular basis is that people just start to expect it. You're supposed to win the state championship every year, or in their eyes, the season was a failure. No one wants to hear about the talent level of the kids falling off or coaching changes. They don't believe it; just like they wouldn't believe the whole mess we had just been through finally resulted in the state championship.

We won the conference again in wrestling, so it was business as usual, and then came the 2003 school year.

Football was on its way again too, with another successful season on the horizon. It was a record turn-out this year. You know how it is in life, everyone wants to be part of a winner; big part or small part, everyone wants to win. So during the 2003 season, win we did. We went into the 2003 state championship again, this time undefeated, with some leftover starts from the last state championship and some new JV graduates ready to make themselves a name on the varsity squad. So the Cavaliers found themselves in a familiar place. They had already won the conference and western regional championship and were once again playing for the state championship. This time, the setting would be the home field of North Carolina State University in Raleigh, North Carolina. The opponent would be the Southwest Onslow Stallions. Guess what? They had defeated our old opponents, the Clinton Dark Horses, during the year, to become the dominant power in eastern North Carolina, at least for 2003.

I've been blessed to have coached many young men in my career of forty years. I've always felt the same about each and every one of them. I mean, as if they were my own kids. I tried to treat them the same way I would want my own kids to be treated if they were coached by somebody else. Every now and then, there are some kids that just need more than other kids—attention, discipline, care, guidance, and love. We had one special kid on this team as we readied ourselves to play for our third championship. We will call him Robert for the sake of anonymity. Robert would play a big part in Cummings athletics during his upcoming year.

We'll get back to Robert later. But for now, let's get back to the state championship. Could the Cavaliers pull off back-to-back championships? It would be a great feat in that only a few teams have done it in history. Once again, it's gonna be a bruising, running game, a big stingy defense on their part, with a vaunted passing attack with our 1,000-yard rusher transfer still in the backfield for his senior year.

We had studied game films for about a week. The South West Onslow Stallions showed us one defense, but somewhere in our gut, we had the feeling that they had discussed the situation with our old friends, the Clinton Dark Horses. Remember, they were just down the road from each other, and we thought Clinton might had given them a little help during the week. I still felt like they had the feeling they had let one get away for them a year earlier.

The stage was set, with us getting first chance on offense. The huge quick Stallion linemen provided us with problems; it was hard to comprehend on film. They came at us hard, every play with different twists and stunts that made them a terror to block. Our athletic quarterback, who had taken over the same position his brother had occupied a few years earlier, was a leading athlete. He could pull the ball down on a pass play and turn and cover receivers into a long running play by himself.

This is one of the most difficult things to defend as a high school defensive coordinator, and believe me, I know, I've been one. But to this point, this season, we hadn't met a defensive line quite like this one. The Southwest Onslow Stallions pursued every play straight up the field, fighting through there would-be blockers staging in lanes they left, no running lanes for our shifty-nifty all-state quarterback or our 1,000-yard rusher of that year—our star running back.

So our agile quarterback, who usually broke a game open, found himself swarmed or running for his life. The Stallions had taken a page out of our old school friend's playbook, the Clinton Dark Horses—simply throwing it if you think you can and throw we would when we could. We made the decision to throw a lot of underneath passes since we had dropped some long ones or just misconnected on some, which were out of reach, but connect on them we did.

The rush up front was tenacious. On the ensuing drive on a particular play, the South West Onslow noseguard knocked our center a backward flip in the air. You don't see that very often in a high school game.

But let's blow our own horn some. Our boy, Robert, who we mentioned earlier, terrorized people all year and continued to do so during this game. He had something like twelve tackles at halftime and would go on to be a college standout at Hibbons University of Minnesota and Western Kentucky. Both of our linebackers, Durrell Mapp and one we'll call the Grinch, were dogged. Mapp would go on to start at the University of North Carolina at Chapel Hill. He would be the player of the week many times in the ACC.

Halftime arrived with Southwest Onslow entering the locker room with a touchdown lead. For the first time at Cummings since we had been there, we entered the locker room with nothing on the scoreboard at halftime.

Only our colleague Frank Mensch had ever seen Cummings with 0 at halftime. He used to tell us the stories. I've been here when we were 10–0, and I've been here when we were 16–0. Coach Mensch had been there since the school's inception in 1970. In the early years, Cummings played in the 4-A division and did it with a JV squad, since Cummings had no juniors or seniors.

We went to the locker room down but not out. We had our chance but seemingly done a lot to ourselves with dropped passes and the inability to mount a running game. That would allow them to pin their ears back on the pass rush. The sheer physical aspect was starting to take a toll. Our noseguard Robert sat in his cubicle smoldering. Then, after the coaches had talked to the separate groups and to the team, Robert could hold it in no longer. He stood out of his cubicle and said, "Y'all be reading the paper too much. These big white boys up front are killing y'all." He was right. He said a few other things all positive after that to get his team cranked up.

The Cavaliers took the field for the second half, scoreless for the first time since any of us could remember. One adjustment at the half had been to keep playing defense as we had been. After all, we had done the same thing to them they had been doing to us on offense. The only difference was their front four were pounding us, except for our noseguard Robert and our two linebackers, Mapp and the Grinch, who were wreaking havoc.

We got the ball first, drove down the field throwing short underneath passes, and scored in the first series to open up the second half. We kicked the extra point and took the lead, but it was not to be. Somewhere in the third quarter, we ran a stunt where the kids got confused. While both of them occupied the same gap, off tackle was left open, and one of their huge running backs sprang through that gap. We gave chase but couldn't catch him. Once again, we found ourselves behind. An unfamiliar position for us, being that we were undefeated on the year with that high-powered passing attack we could score from anywhere and at any time.

Try as we might, we could not pull it out. Dropped passes as a matter of fact, we dropped a pass on the last possession of the game just outside the ten-yard line that could have been a touchdown. The clock expired, and there was that terrible feeling again.

After all that hard work, we were 15 and 1, a record that any team in the state would be happy to possess. Our noseguard Robert cried uncontrollably in the middle of the field while holding on to Coach Eddie Foust. Others were on a knee in the middle of the field with their heads down, unable to believe it. As they handed out the run-ner-up trophy, it was not to be our day. But this team with its one loss would be remembered for many of its outstanding players and plays. Our shifty-nifty quarter-back, Bo, would go on to play at the alma mater for all of us, Elon University.

You know about Mapp and Robert. Already, our running back and 1,000-yard rusher would sign a schol-arship with Marshall University. Our two receivers would later play college football as well.

So what looked like a missed opportunity became a great memory for some and an extension of opportunities for others. No, it wasn't business as usual for the coaching staff. We worked just as hard as we always had. We drove the kids to become better students, athletes, and most importantly, good citizens. But at the same time, we realized we had been to the state championship three times in three consecutive years.

Now we all fully realized that there are football teams all over the state and this country that work very hard every day and have never had the privilege of playing in a state championship game. I am talking about in their entire lives. As all of us coaches, Johnson, Perdue, Mensch, Foust, McCauley, Shepherd, and I realized that if you work as hard as you can, you must have talent, but even with all that, you still must have a little luck to win a state championship. If it were easy, the same teams would win it every year. I have watched many teams who I thought superior be eliminated in the layoffs for one reason or another.

Now we're back to that nervousness and fear of the unknown that was mentioned earlier. Our JV team continued to be successful for which I feel especially proud. After all, my trainees had one many back-to-back conference championships. The JVs had continued their ways into winning conference championships while on the varsity team, playing in three and winning one of them. Our wrestling team also continued to be successful, of which I will talk later.

But for now, are the Cavaliers done football-wise? Let's see. The school year of 2004 would roll around. We had gotten used to going to the state championship game and had hoped this year would bring the same. As mentioned before, the expectations by the Cavalier fans and community already felt that if we didn't win the state championship, then it wasn't a productive season.

In 2004, our football fortunes would stay intact as we would advance to the semifinals of the state tournament. There we'd play Shelby High School of Hickory, North Carolina. We had played Shelby before in the playoffs many times. It was always an exciting game, and we'd managed to win most of them.

Here we were in Hickory, North Carolina, on a cold Friday night, to see who would eventually play our old friends, the Southwest Onslow Stallions. They had again proven dominant on the eastern NC coastal plains. We had our shifty-nifty quarterback, Bo, before his eventual departure to Elon, and two great receivers, coupled with a running back who would eventually sign with Wake Forest University. Besides our quarterback mentioned earlier, we had a future University of North Carolina start and future New England Patriot's wide receiver Brandon Tate. As if that wasn't enough, we had another receiver, T. J. Gwynn, who had played football and basketball all his life. After an almost career-ending AAU injury during summer basketball, he had decided to concentrate on just basketball since that was going to be his area of concentration in college.

TJ would later sign with Commonwealth University in Virginia, but not before he carried the bacon along with his teammate Brandon Tate in this particular football game. Several days before summer practice, TJ changed his mind, suddenly unfearful of an already-injured knee. He said, after thinking it over, that he wanted to play and couldn't stand the thought of letting his teammates down.

So he put on his knee brace and led us along with these other champion teammates to where we were now, one game away from the state championship.

Shelby had always been a formidable opponent, winning several championships themselves, and on this night, it would be no different. It was 21–0 at the half once again, and our future starts remembered an old adage of mine, "Big-time players step up in big-time games," and so they did with only minutes gone at the beginning of the second half.

Our big gun, Brandon Tate, helped tie the score with an electrifying kickoff and punt returns to open up the second half. Along with a touchdown catch by T. J. Gwynn, we had done in minutes what it had taken Shelby a whole half to do, score twenty-one points.

As the game wound on, we'd become victim to another great running attack offered up by Shelby. This time, however, it seemed to be more of a finessed, slashing type of attack, not the bruising encounters when we had gotten this far before.

As fate reared its ugly head again, we'd come up short at the end of the game, losing in the semifinals. After all, we'd beaten them a lot more than they'd beaten us in the past. That still didn't seem to help somehow. That feeling always seems to gather within you. Not just disappointment but a season-kind of flashing before your eyes at a steady speed, coupled with the inner knowledge of how hard it had been to get there.

Well, back to that missed-opportunity thing again. We'd still have some great memories with some of the fantastic young people we'd been allowed to coach. Brandon Tate would go out and lead the NCAA in kickoff and punt returns and a pro career. TJ would be a basketball star at Virginia Commonwealth, and shifty-nifty Bo, our quarterback, would become an Elon champion. Pretty good year after all.

Winning is important, but here again, as mentioned earlier, giving the kids the best possible experience is what counts. That means what everyone who's ever been successful in coaching or teaching knows about, self-sacrifice. By sacrifice, I mean all those long hours away from your own family. It's hard to explain to your family how you are able to spend more time with someone else's kids than you do your own. Or when you average out the basic coach's salary in NC by dividing the number of hours you spent this season by the amount they pay you, it's about twenty-five cents per hour. By sacrifice, I mean loaning a kid sitting on a bus alone some money after an away game or match for which he brought no money, probably because his family didn't have it. By sacrifice, I mean sitting on a curb in front of a school while several of our athletes wait on their rides. By sacrifice, I mean giving a kid a ride home after practice, and upon arrival, there are four cars sitting in the driveway of the kid you're taking home.

By sacrifice, I mean going to all those summer camps and doing fund-raisers to pay for camp and doing fund-raisers before and after camps are over. Late nights, cold suppers, and the list goes on. Now you can ask me again the title of this book, Coach, are you crazy? Even though the awards seem few as compared to the list of costs above, it goes beyond winning and losing. Don't get me wrong. After all those years of winning, I still get a tingle. But the real payoff comes in watching those superathletes we've coached go on to do tremendous things with their lives. That's the real payoff. Some need more help than others just as we all do at times.

Now we can momentarily return to our noseguard, Robert, from the football team. He was also an all-conference all-state wrestler and standout track performer. He was a guy who seemingly never met a stranger and loved his community and everyone in it.

Robert was a kid who sometimes struggled academically but never on the athletic field. Robert never battled with character but on occasion was somewhat bad-tempered. However, hanging around the coaches, we all felt that we had a part in his formation. As a person, he learned to control his temperament and use his energy for more productive things.

Many weekends I spent with Robert, not just playing football or all-day wrestling tournaments, but working on my farm or mowing yards or cutting firewood. Robert would work with me to make money to buy things he needed or sometimes even to pay for summer school.

Robert was a businessman. He carried this large backpack with him everywhere. One day, in my science class, of which Robert was a member, I called the roll, looking at each student. As I did so, I turned to look at the board to point at what today's lesson would be. I then turned to face the students, and everyone had a cold canned soft drink on their desk. Since this had never happened before and was against school policy, I forcefully inquired, "What are y'all doing? Where did those drinks come from?" Smiling boldly, they all pointed to Robert.

See, it wasn't till later that I discovered Robert had placed some large sandwich bags inside his book bag. He then went to Food Lion and bought twenty or thirty very cheap sodas. He placed them in his book bag and sold them for twice what he paid for them. Robert was a businessman or a survivor; some might say a finagler.

We used to watch Robert approach someone in the hall and ask to borrow a dollar, and when they both opened their wallets, Robert had more money than the guy he borrowed the dollar from. However, he always paid his debts, mostly from the money he got working for me. We'd also watched Robert prevent other students from picking on classmates even before we could get there to stop it.

Robert was a teammate everyone admired for his honesty, effort, athleticism, and work ethic. He won many a football game for us and many a wrestling match. I remember in the state wrestling tournament on one occasion, Robert was nearing the finals. As he peered over at a large lineman from Swain County, a usual football powerhouse in the NC mountains, he suddenly got quiet as he beheld this gigantic opponent. Looking up at people staring over the rails and yelling in the Lawrence Joel Coliseum in Winston-Salem, Robert turned to me and said, "Coach, is that the biggest white boy you've ever seen?"

I replied, "That's the biggest white anything I've ever seen."

He then burst into laughter along with me. That seemed to ease the tension as I told him, "You don't worry about it, just stay with our game plan."

Robert won that match. I was terribly uneasy, you know, that fear of the unknown again; however, Robert advanced, finally finishing third. It was quite an accomplishment, after all, the guy Robert had just beat had one of those barbed-wire tattoos on an upper arm that was bigger than my thigh. Nothing changed. Robert continued to amaze us all throughout his high school life. He went on to play football at Western Kentucky and is now a successful businessman.

Back in the school year of 2006, we skipped 2005 to get to the highlights of what was going to be the high point in the Cavalier football fortunes. In 2006, another cross-town transfer from my alma mater, Graham High School, would enter the Cavalier camp.

This guy moves in as a senior. Don't worry. He got doubly scrutinized, and we even talked with our colleagues at Graham. They said he didn't want to conform to playing certain positions that they had requested, so he wound up at our school. The Graham coaches agreed it was best for everyone, especially since he had moved into our district.

Armed with some more of my JV starts and this new, energetic running back, we set out on a quest for another state championship. Wherever this new running back went, he went wide open. He was a pleasure to coach, even on blocking drills, which most running backs hate. He would often knock the dummy holder and the dummy over.

This young man ran the ball as hard as I've ever seen it run. He was a real pleasure to coach. A young quarterback we had been grooming from the JV squad would begin at quarterback and become a true start in his own right. We would tear through the season, and guess what? We wound up back in the state championship again. Our new back was a terror, but it took him awhile to learn the plays. We had instructed our junior quarterback to remind our new running back what to do as we approached the line each time.

One day, at practice, we were running some pass plays during live scrimmage, and we approached the line of scrimmage in a spread formation or the shotgun formation. The running back as usual set off to one side; as soon as the ball was snapped, our new back went the wrong way, ran into the quarterback, causing him to be buried under a mountain of giant humanity. As our junior quarterback, who I admired very much, lay on the ground with only his head protruding faceup from the bottom of the pile, I leaned over looking down at him while he lay pinned there and said, "You've got to tell him every time, every time."

With a big grin on his face, he said, "Get them off of me."

There were a lot of remarkable kids on this team; not one seemed to be pulling in a different direction. Now don't get me wrong. Each team takes on its own personality, especially as the season goes on. This group seemed to be permanently focused. It made coaching much easier. After an impressive season and some exciting playoff wins, the stage was set yet again for another state championship.

So we made it to the state championship in 2006. Guess who our opponents were? Yeah, the Clinton Dark Horses. They had been fighting back and forth in eastern NC for some time in the 2-A division with Southwest Onslow for supremacy, with Clinton winning out this year. This was not, however, like the Clinton teams of old. They had a running game but not that usual bruising attack with sometimes two running backs doing equal damage. They had even lost their first two or three games but came back and took care of business the rest of the season. We, on the other hand, had a running attack from the spread offense that was crushing and pretty much unheard of. After all, the spread, as we still call it at Cummings, is designed for a passing attack with a little run mixed in.

The summer before this season, however, our entire coaching staff packed up and went to the University of Nevada at Las Vegas. The purpose of the trip was to learn more about how to run the ball effectively from the spread offense. So off to Vegas we went. It was a notable trip and probably one of the keys to our successful season.

The attitude at Cummings is that football, like any other sport, is ever-changing. You must change with it or get left behind. And so ever since I'd been there, that's what we did. The stage was set again, this time at Wake Forest University. We felt kinda good because that's where we won our last state championship.

We took the field as the western conference champs, and on the other side, our old buddies the Clinton Dark Horses, who, by this time, were on their third head coach. No pressure over there, huh?

We controlled the game from the start. Our pounding running game left black jerseys lying in our wake. Clinton made a run right before the half, but it was our day, as we came out in the second and built our lead to a 49–20 victory.

Headlines read, RUNAWAY VICTORY, with a picture of our running back breaking into the clear on the front page of the newspaper. By the way, our star, we'll call him Jamal, scored six touchdowns in the game. He was named the MVP on offense, I'd say, for a good reason.

The Cavs had won the 2006 state championship. No empty feelings this time. No, "this one got away," none of that. The Clinton coach, being very complimentary, stated in the paper that he thought he knew something about running the ball until today. Now he really knew something about running the ball.

After the awards ceremony and talking to well-wishers, we took our traveling show back to Burlington. Two second-place finishes in a six-year period? Not bad, huh?

In 2007, we'd reach the third round before bowing out of the playoffs, and in 2008, we went out of the playoffs in the third round. What about 2008? Well, that didn't go as hoped, but what about 2009 or 2010? My money was on the Cavaliers to once again mount a charge to the state championship. Of course, our old foes will still be out there with their own championship aspirations, Clinton, Southwest Onslow, Reidsville, Shelby, and then there is always that surprise team that comes from nowhere and marches into the championship.

That's why they play the game. Good luck to everybody.

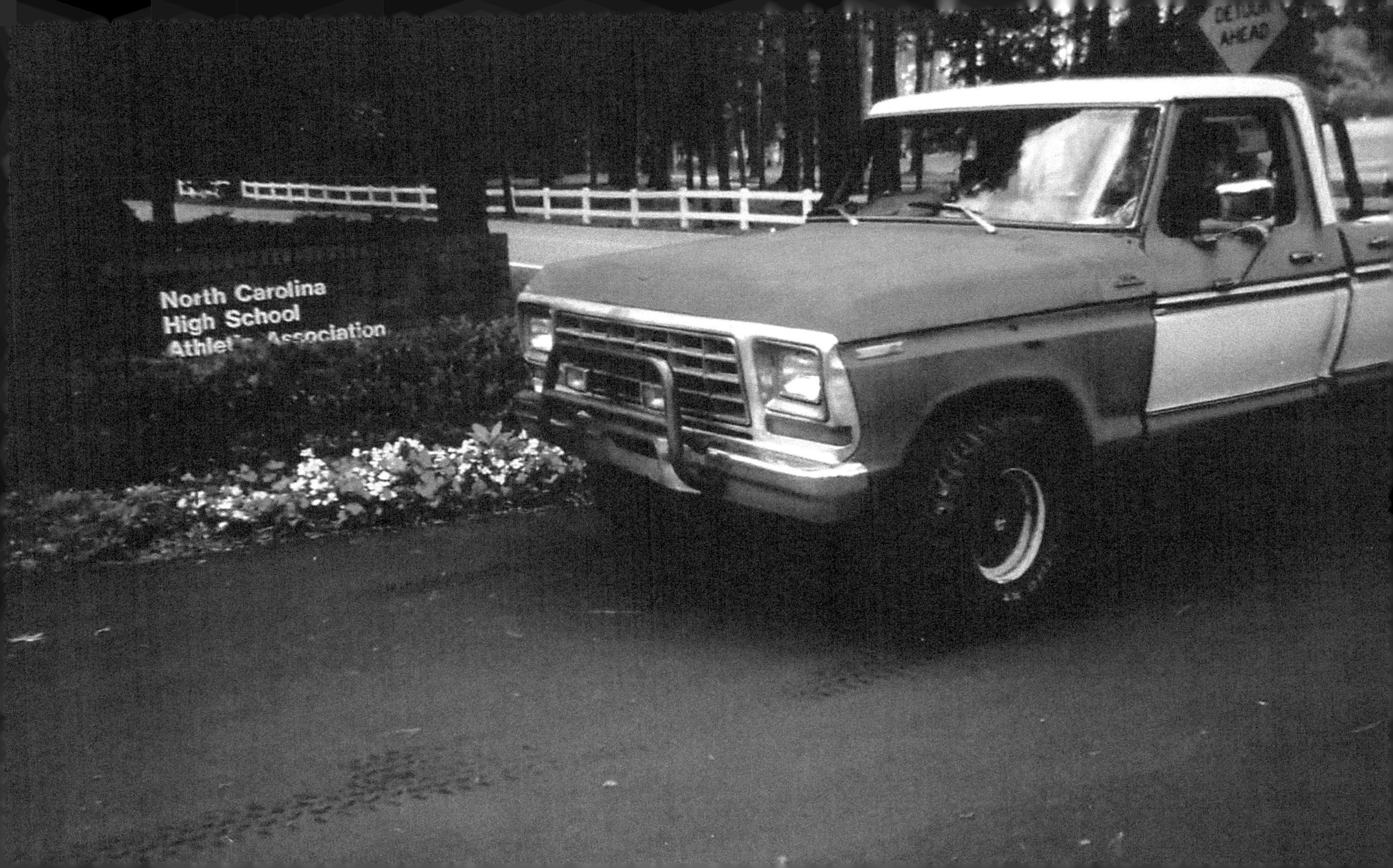
North Carolina
High School
Association
DETOUR
AHEAD

es bring gridiron greatness BY KIMBERLY HAYES '05

Back row l-r: Eddie Foust '80, Johnny Isley '94, Steve Johnson '83 and Frank Mensch '70.
Front row l-r: Andy Hawks '77, Jay Perdue '87, Brent Shepherd and Danny McCawley '93.

ms ation heir

raring lood that peo-

nat it

have a We

treat each other like brothers, and that's been a blessing for us and the team."

McCawley agrees.

"Good professors helped prepare me to teach, so when I started I was prepared," says McCawley, who is also head baseball coach at Cummings. "I was also able to start coaching while I was at Elon."

One professor in particular had a lasting impact on the group.

"Dr. Janie Brown was a huge influence of mine," says Perdue, who is also the school's athletics director. "I began my coaching career

under her husband, coach Mickey Brown, at Western Alamance High School. He was a former Elon football coach in the 1970s and was my greatest influence in the beginning."

Mensch is a legend of sorts at Cummings. After graduating from Elon, he got a job hauling bricks as part of the construction of the high school, which is a 15-minute drive from Elon's campus. Later he taught physical education at Cummings and has coached football, baseball, wrestling, tennis and track.

"I've been at Cummings when we were 0-10 and when we were 15-0," says Mensch. "I'm ready for retirement, but I'm still having fun."

Mensch will always be grateful to Elon for giving him a good education.

"I've had a lot of great friends from Elon who I've coached with and against," he says.

Says Johnson, "It's nice to say everyone on the staff is an Elon graduate. We all like wearing Elon stuff and attending Elon games. We're very proud of the university."

Teacher finds hard work has rewards

By SHARON SMITH
Times-News

Andy Hawks is no stranger to hard work.

And for the last two decades, he's been passing his love of labor on to his students.

Hawks, a biology teacher, wrestling coach and assistant football coach at Cummings High School, has been selected Dickies' 1996 American worker of the year. And as part of his award, Hawks will appear on ABC's Good Morning America show this morning.

Representatives from the Texas clothing manufacturer told Hawks the good news a week ago. The 41-year-old educator said he was stunned.

"I said, 'I don't know what you're talking about,'" he said. "I've never won anything in my life."

Please see REWARDS / A7

But Kristen Kauffman, spokeswoman for Dickies, said the award was no joke. She said Hawks was chosen as one of the company's two national winners. The other winner is a female construction worker from Georgia.

Kauffman said the folks at Dickies received thousands of entries from across the country, but a 75-word essay written by Dana Albright about her fellow teacher really stood out.

"He was not just a hard worker himself," Kauffman said. "But he seemed to be passing on his work ethic to young people."

What the Alamance County native has been doing is hiring impoverished students to work with him at his side business, Andy's Wood Service. He said he picks the students up and pays them $7 an hour to do fix-up work.

"We sell firewood, fix pipes, mow grass — high class stuff," ...

money to send his students to wrestling camp. So, Hawks' athletes went to work to pay for their trip to Boone.

"They painted two houses," he said. "They got the money and everybody went."

Hawks, who has been a teacher at various schools throughout the state for the past 23 years, said he got the idea for his business when he got his first teacher's paycheck. He said it was $600 for a month's work.

"I had a house payment," he said. "Good God, my house payment was more than that."

Hawks said he started doing fix-up work to pay bills and to afford extras. After many years in the teaching profession, Hawks said, he's now making somewhere around $30,000.

"It isn't in the driving a Cadillac range," he said.

But, he said, it allows him to concentrate more on his students' ability to pay their bills

personal use.

Hawks, who said he likes to travel, is also going to the Grand Ole Opry in Nashville on Sept. 20. There he will take center stage, where he will be awarded a plaque for his efforts.

Kauffman said that's just a taste of some of the benefits of being selected a national winner.

"It's exciting," she said.

"They are subject to a photo shoot of them at work which goes into the Dickies' Worker's Choice catalog. They become cover models."

Winners are also invited to Fort Worth, Texas, for a party at Dickies, where they will get to mingle with everyone from the company's receptionist to the president while feasting on Texas barbecue.

Kauffman said this is the fifth year the company has held the contest. She said it's Dickies' way of saying thanks to the

CHAPTER 10

Not Iron

So the 2008 season was underway with my JV team humming as well as the varsity. My biology classes were going well, nothing out of the ordinary. I felt as usual, not overly tired or sick or the like.

One October morning I awoke, ate a big breakfast, and went to school, arriving about 7:30 AM. I went by the coaches' office to pick at and give my colleagues a little grief. As time went on, I went up to check my school mailbox and then on to my classroom.

The bell rang, and my students began to enter the room as I picked at them, and they responded in good humor. That would be the last thing I would remember for four days. Except for blurry bits and pieces. I collapsed right behind my desk. Although I don't remember it, I'd got off the floor and collapsed again. The students at first thought I was picking at them, then realized something was terribly wrong.

As I lay on the floor, one of my students ran out the door and entered the office, yelling, "Something's wrong with Coach Hawks. He just fell out!" The assistant principal, Mr. Emmitt Alexander, called 911 and told them of the situation and alerted everyone else. An entourage of concerned dear friends and colleagues converged on my room. The kids were shuttled off to another room for their benefit.

Only minutes had passed before my coach family had gathered or, rather, ran to my rescue. I was completely blue from the waist up. As my friends tore my newest dress shirt from my torso, Coach Eddie Foust began to pump on my chest while Coach Steve Johnson began giving me mouth-to-mouth resuscitation while Coaches Perdue, Shepherd, and Mr. Alexander talked to me, trying to help me hang on to a thread of life. These dear friends were doing me a bigger favor than just keeping me alive; they were keeping oxygen flowing to my brain, preventing almost inevitable brain damage, since my heart had stopped beating completely.

Coach Foust pumped on my chest, sobbing all the while until he finally collapsed himself. Immediately, Coach Johnson and Coach Mensch replaced him. Finally, the EMTs arrived about thirty minutes after they had been called. I was shocked on the spot with one of those defibrillators and revived. But for all intents and purposes, I had died right there on the very job I loved.

It was painless, effortless, just like somebody turned off a light switch.

I was rushed immediately to the local hospital, Alamance Regional, where I spent the next several hours. In the meantime, Coach Perdue, and an old friend, Chad Cook, went to do the unenviable task of telling my mother. Upon arrival at my mother's house, they knocked on the door. When my mother answered and Coach Perdue said, crying, "Mrs. Hawks, Andy has collapsed at school, I think he's dying, and they have taken him to the hospital." My mother in solemn face said, "Wait a minute till I put on my shoes."

Upon arrival at the hospital, I had been unconscious the entire time as immediate family and well-wishers came and gathered outside. They informed my mother that I had a massive heart attack and probably wouldn't be here much longer, so she had better go in and speak to me.

My mother went in and asked the attendants after viewing me with a large hose protruding from my mouth and nose. "What are you doing?" They responded they had done pretty much everything they could do. She became angry and informed them to send me to Duke or Chapel Hill medical centers. They told her I wouldn't make the trip. She replied, "He's not going to lie here and die while you're drinking our coffee."

So shipped me they did, by helicopter, on the Life Flight from Burlington to Durham right into Duke Medical Center. I missed probably one of the greatest views of my life by being unconscious. The real irony is they passed right over my farm. It would have been a kick to see it from the air.

I awoke three days later with a very young doctor looking into one of my eyes. I asked him, "Are you the guy in charge?"

He said, "Yep."

"You mean I'm not dead?"

He said "No, but you scared all of us."

I asked him what had happened. "Did I have a heart attack or something?"

He said, "No, we checked every blood vessel in your body while you were out, and you have not one blockage anywhere. That's very unique, especially for a man of your age. If you don't have any blockage by now, it is not likely you will have one."

Of course, my next question for the doctor was, What had caused all this? He went on to inform me that my heart was larger than it should be, much larger. After looking at my medical history, he had determined the same diagnosis I had received in Greensboro fifteen years earlier. You remember the death sentence with a prognosis of a year and a half to live? My problem seemed to result from pneumonia contracted from a cold in the

1980s. Cardiomyopathy is the medical term for it, but ultimately, my heart was so big that on this special day, October 2007, the electrical impulse that makes all our hearts beat so many times a minute struck a spot of scar tissue, and my heart didn't respond or stopped beating. You know, it's funny how all of us take those little everyday occurrences within our bodies for granted until they stop.

The doctor and I then had a conversation where I asked him, "Will this occur again? You know, where my electrical impulse strikes a dead zone or scar tissue and just goes dead again."

He answered, "Yes. It could be ten days or ten years or ten minutes, but it will happen again."

I then replied, "So I gotta walk around the rest of my life waiting for the other shoe to drop?"

He quickly smiled along with his reply and said, "With some special surgery, I can fix it."

So I then energetically asked, "Why didn't you do it while I was asleep those first three days?"

Again smiling, he said, "We've got to run some more tests first. We also had to have your permission."

So the next several days, I was under heavy observation at Duke University Medical Center. I hope you never have to go to a hospital in your entire life, but if you do, you will never receive better care anywhere. There are probably some places comparable, but not better.

The doctor visited me daily while I built my strength for their fix-all surgery coming up. I was under some heavy medication. At one point upon waking up, I was seeing a bed full of snakes crawling all over me, my worst fear. Upon summoning the nurse, she informed me and my visitors that it was a reaction to the drug I was being given intravenously to speed my recovery. The drug supposedly brought out your worst fears as it was administered. They certainly made a believer out of me. The next morning, the young doctor entered my room while I was still in intensive care and said, "There have been hundreds of visitors in the waiting room for the past several days." Many of those wonderful folks and dear friends passed through while I was unconscious. I just want to *thank all of you from the bottom of my heart.*

The doctor also said the switchboard had registered hundreds of calls from all over North Carolina and other states as well, all inquiring about my condition. The doctor said jokingly, "You must be a pretty important guy."

I replied laughingly, "Well, maybe I had done something right."

The doctor then turned serious and said, "Andy, you were out a very long time, and we're worried that you might have suffered some brain damage due to the lack of oxygen. Would you mind me asking you some questions?"

Of course, my reply was, "No." I then said, "Doc, a lot of people might say I lost a lot of oxygen to my brain a long time ago, but go ahead."

He said, "You used to have two saddle horses, which you loved very much. What were their names?"

I immediately said, "Sam and Elvira."

Sam was a big Appaloosa I'd had for many years. Elvira was a black Tennessee walking horse, a mare that my grandfather and I had saved from death. Her owner simply gave her to us, not wanting to dig a hole that big when she died. We nursed her back to health. She and Sam gave many of my students, my grandfather, and me many years of pleasure, riding throughout the trails here in Alamance County.

The doctor said after I shared that memory, "These are supposed to be short answers."

I told him to go ahead with the questions. The doctor then asked, "What is the nickname for your red pickup truck?"

I replied, "The Mule," of which he laughed now and said, "I hear and have already found out that you are quite a joker. Tell me a joke, one that takes more than two sentences."

"Doc, this young man was getting into a lot of trouble back in the old days, so his father took him to a local monastery. He then proceeded to inform the head monk that he would like to leave him there to get straightened out. He reaffirmed he was out of control and a detriment to the community. The head monk agreed, reinforcing the father's position to the young man that no nonsense would be tolerated. The father left his son at the monastery. The head monk then began to explain what he expected from him, to stay in the monastery and eventually become a monk himself.

"The head monk told the young man he'd first have to take a vow of silence. He'd have to move about the compound at the monastery without speaking a word to anyone for an entire week. So the young man set out to do just that. After a week's time, the head monk called the young man into his office. He congratulated him on completing his task. He told the young man, 'You went around the entire week without speaking a word, congratulations.'

"Next the head monk informed the young man he'd have to take a vow of fasting. He would have to go about the compound all week without food. So the young man once again set about his task. In a week, the head monk was congratulating his new pupil. The head monk told him he was two-thirds of the way to his goal.

"The next task for the young man would be the doing of charitable deeds. He would have to move about the upcoming week in the compound of the monastery doing virtuous deeds. The catch was he could not receive the gifts or nominal rewards for doing the good deeds.

As a matter of fact, he couldn't take anything for helping those in the monastery.

"At the end of the third week, the young man was called in by the head monk and was congratulated for achieving all three of the difficult tasks. He was now accepted into the monastery as a full-fledged monk.

"The elated young man was then walked across the street by the head monk to be shown his vocation to best serve the Lord. They walked to the top of a huge bell tower. A large bell awaited them with a schedule on the wall. The young monk was informed he'd have to pull the rope to ring the bell every hour on the hour to let the other members of the community know what time it was, so they could perform certain tasks and prayers, serving God. The head monk walked down the spiral staircase leading from the bell tower. Suddenly the young monk looked on the schedule and realized it was time to ring the bell. He pulled the rope so hard that it broke. The bell flung back and hit the young monk on the forehead.

"The bell rang unbelievably loudly as it never had before. The old head monk raced up the steps to the top of the bell tower elatedly, telling the young monk on his arrival that the bell had never rang so loudly before. 'Keep up the excellent work,' he told the young monk. The young man couldn't bear to tell him that he'd broken the rope, so the rest of the day, every time the bell needed to be rung, he'd merely hit it with his head. After all, the rope was broken. By the end of the day, however, the new monk's head was black and blue. Suddenly, the time came for the bell to be rung for the last time that day.

"So painfully, the young monk reared back and hit his forehead on the bell one last time. The pain was so bad, the young monk grabbed his forehead, and as he stumbled around in the bell tower, he fell out of the window, crashing to the ground.

"Suddenly the other monks gathered, pointing at the various body parts lying on the ground. One monk called, 'Oh, look, there's an arm,' and another monk yelled, 'There's a leg!' Another monk asked if anyone knew his name. One monk yelled, 'No, but his face rings a bell!'"

The doctor looked at me and said, "That could possibly be one of the worst jokes I have ever heard. But obviously, my friend, there is nothing wrong with your long-term or short-term memory. You're a very lucky man not just to have your brain intact but to be alive."

I responded by reassuring him, "Don't I know it?"

The young doctor went on to inform me he'd had a discussion with my regular cardiologist, Dr. Kirkwood Adams from Chapel Hill.

He went on to say that he and his staff were very concerned. His exact words were, "Don't let anything happen to him. He's a special one." The young doctor at Duke said, "We're quickly understanding it. He'll be okay after the surgery."

So during the next several days, I greeted well-wishers and friends as I prepared myself for the surgery. One night while lying there in bed at Duke University Medical Center, in the wee hours of the morning, unable to sleep, my mind began to wander. As I looked up at the ceiling, I began to speak to God, hoping that he was still up. Basically, the conversation was, *I know I'm still here for a reason. Please give me some type of sign, and I'll do my best to fulfill those wishes. If it's what I've been doing, then grant me a speedy recovery, and I'll do my best to finish it out as I began.* Okay, you can all ask the title of the book again, Coach, are you crazy? I'd just had a major health and personal setback, and I'm thinking about continuing as if nothing bad had happened. I had asked the Lord to send me some type of sign as to why I was still here. Guess what? The very next day, Coach Perdue, the other coaches, and Chad Cook brought in this humongous box. They put it down in my room on the floor.

Of course, my first question was, "What is that?"

Coach Perdue replied, "It's a box full of cards and letters from all the kids at school, some who have graduated and other teachers and family and of course friends from the community."

God had sent me my message and not too subtly either. So I made up my mind right then and there to spend the rest of my life just as I'd spent the beginning, trying to help the kids. After a very painful surgery and a loss of about thirty pounds, the day would come for me to get out of the hospital, three weeks later. For those wondering about the rehabilitation process, one of the weakest moments of my life was about to spring itself on me.

After all, I'd been a high school and college athlete; I'd been a champion at both. I was a physical farm boy and logger who had never backed down from anything. I'd made up my mind I'd not back down now. I'd have to admit I'd never been weaker in my life. One time, waiting in my cardiologist's examining room, he allowed me to catch a glimpse at my medical records.

When you see a patient die a sudden cardiac death, it has a very sobering effect on you. One thing I'd learned from my friend Dr. Kirkwood Adams was don't let this disease dictate you; you dictate it. Carry on a normal life just as you had before. I don't think he understood as many did not know how discouraging and difficult it was to carry around this heavy weight, but then maybe he did.

In any event, I refused to let this problem become debilitating, to keep from reaching any goal I had set for myself now or for the future. So my good friend Chad Cook gave me a ride home from the hospital. As I waited out front, I looked at the reflection of the clothes I had on as they flapped in the wind. I looked into that large stained-glass window, cheeks sunken in, and I thought, *Wow, this is going to be a battle.*

One of the most special people I've ever met nursed me back to health. While I was in the hospital, she slept in two chairs beside my bed, and when I returned to my country home, she slept in the room next to mine. She'd sometimes jump up in the middle of the night when I would have coughing spells. She is a nurse by profession, and she showered her labor of love on me. I'm talking about Miriam Lopez.

You think you're thankful until you really gauge how many people played a part in your still being around. All the football coaches who were there for me: Steve Johnson, Eddie Foust, Jay Perdue, Brent Shepherd, Frank Mensch, and my good friend, Chad Cook. Then, all the nurses and doctors, paramedics, and so forth. Then there are the kids that ran to get help. Then at the end there was Miriam Lopez, nurse exemplified.

If you ever want to talk about luck, then you can come and talk to me. To have all these wonderful, caring people in my life, then to have them all play a grand part in one of the most tragic days I've been involved with up to now, it's a miracle. I'm not a religious person, don't get me wrong. I am a believer. I just don't go around spouting my beliefs. Okay, at least not on that particular subject. But if you don't believe in miracles, just like I said before, you can come and talk to me. My grandmother told me one time that when she was a relatively young woman, she was diagnosed with breast cancer, and then soon after surgery, it showed up again. At a youthful age, she had been through more pain, agony, and fear than most people face in their entire lives.

We had many discussions of which I treasure every single one today. She told me when she was first diagnosed with cancer, her immediate thought was what will happen to Ellen and Sidney (my aunt and father), her two young children? Now this elderly woman could tell her story due to skilled doctors (especially in that time and that tenacity to stay alive) for her young children's sake.

She lived a noble life, and we were blessed to have her to an old age. So armed with that same tenacity, I continued my fight with heart disease, vowing to live a full, successful, and service-filled life.

One of the stories I remember most from my grandmother was when she said she was lying in the hospital thinking how terrible things were, especially to be such a young person having to cope with these struggles. She reminded me of a visit by her and my grandfather's pastor. A country minister from the Virginia Mountains (Jim Vass), who told my grandmother, Tacey, no matter how bad it seems, look around you, and you can always find someone in worse shape than yourself. To this day, I cherish those long-ago conversations. I know it might seem silly, but they have more meaning now than ever before. My grandfather in his later years told me it was funny about life. By the time a man learns all he needs to be successful in life, it's too late because you're almost dead. Then cheerfully he said, "Oh well, I guess it goes back to that passage in the Bible, 'Every day a man lives, he grows weaker but wiser.'"

So here I am, a miracle in progress. As I explained earlier, there is a reason I'm still here. After all, how could all the most important people in my life be there to save me? The collisions with death must have occurred at just the right time, instead of maybe an hour earlier when I would have had no help and then at the end. Like that angel of mercy who nursed me back to health.

All this isn't just luck or coincidence; it's a miracle. Don't get me wrong. I don't think of this as some super-hero-type thing. I call it a miracle, and I am destined to do more good. To quote my doctor at Duke, "God isn't through with you yet. You've still got a lot more stuff to do, great stuff like you've already done."

After a very short-breathed, much-needed rest of about a year and a half, I was back at full strength. My doctor still says I might make it into eighties; of course, my reply is, "Doc, don't get carried away." After all, I don't want to live so long, you know, like when I have to wear diapers or something. You know, outliving all your friends. When you start telling stories of the past (repeatedly), and the younger ones think you're hallucinating or something.

At least after this death sentence, with which I had lived all these years (partially lifted), I was ready to go out and pursue my coaching career again. Oh, yeah, while I was in the hospital recovering, an article came out in the newspaper titled, COMEBACK COACH. Guess what? That's not the first time they've had to print that article. But they were right.

I have been coaching again for quite a few years. Well, what can I say, to quote an adage, "I can't sing, and I can't dance." As I said, I don't have as much of the energy as I used to, but I don't think that comes from the heart deal. I think a lot of it comes from age.

Don't ever get it wrong though. I still have the passion for athletics, but I have always had coaching philosophies that might differ from other coaches. To be successful though, they will all agree that their upcoming ideals, when put into place, are the hammer and nails for building a scaffold for success. This goes not only for the coaching and teaching professions, but in all parts of life, personal and professional.

PHILOSOPHIES

1. *Always remember it's all about the kids.* You take care of the kids first. Their best interests, both long and short term, are your responsibility. That means sitting one out of a game because he missed practice to set an example for him and his teammates. To teach them life lessons through team concepts is your responsibility. Never play a kid who is injured just to win a ball game. They don't have self-discipline yet. It's your responsibility to help them develop it. It doesn't make any difference how badly the team needs him or if he's a star or not, and who his father is has nothing to do with it either. It's up to you to make the point with him. You guys who have coached before know what I'm talking about. Maybe not the young ones, but you'll learn at some point. The values your players learn from you may be the last or only consequences they have faced in life up to today. After all, if he skips work one day, he might lose much more than a game or an opportunity to shine. He may lose a job and abil-

ity to support his family. Compassion must be available as well. There may be mitigating circumstances. You need to understand the effects before you hand out consequences to players for misconduct. Don't cut someone's head off, so to speak, for minor infractions. It's a good idea to hand out a rules sheet at the first team meeting you have, then go over it point by point and have them sign it. This way, no one can say, "I didn't know it was a rule." Learn all you can about the sport or class you're teaching. This instills confidence in what you're to do and helps all the kids buy into it. Explain what it is you're trying to accomplish by doing activities which lead to goals.

2. *Be organized.* You get a lot more done in the time you have allotted. It's more fun for everyone, and it's easier in games and practice. Have a time frame; follow it as closely as possible. It's also easier to gauge where you are as far as the overall picture goes. There are fewer discipline problems as well. Be organized but not with too many rules. You can rule yourself right out of efficiency by trying to enforce too many rules.

3. *Be the role model.* No matter what type of environment, socioeconomic background, cities, villages, urban, suburban, or rural, you set the example for your fellow coaches and kids. Kids don't like irony. They like things cut and dried. There's no reason

for me to say, "We're not going to have any of that damn cussing out here," and expect that to be the end of it. You be on time, they'll show up on time. It may take a little while, but it will happen. You must be the first one there and the last one to leave. You must be involved in your community of which you coach in a positive way. You must be a hard worker in anything else to get your fellow coaches excited as well as all the players. It becomes contagious; it rubs off on everybody. One of my motivational speeches includes, "We are going to hit a place or point in this match where they are going to reach down and turn it up a notch. Then we're going to have a turn it up a notch. Then they will turn it up another notch. We may have to then ring off the knob." Always be confident and instill this in your players. Never be cocky. You're just setting yourself and them up for a big fall. Alan Brown, the head football coach at Thomasville, once said, "There are two types of people in this business. The humble and the humbled." No truer words could be spoken, especially for you young folks just getting started in the coaching business.

4. *Hang out with winners.* Make sure the kids hang out with people who have high goals for them as well as themselves. No, you can't pick their friends; it would be futile to try. But emphasize when interacting with them how important it is to hang out with win-

ners. Those who are your real friends want success for you as much as they do for themselves. They are not jealous because they love you and because you're their friend. They trust you and you them, and if this isn't the way it is, you need to separate yourself from those people. And as you coach, associate yourself with winners. You want people who've been successful and those who want success for you, people you can learn from. I know you can't always pick your fellow coaches or colleagues, especially in high school. No one could have been lucky enough to be involved with that winning bunch of fellow football coaches that I have had the honor of being with for the past umpteen years. We're still like brothers today. Not many people are that fortunate. To be around people who are knowledgeable and share the same philosophies you do is especially remarkable. It's pretty significant. We sat down one day at a meeting and figured out our coaching years of experience in football alone. Guess what? It tallied up to be over one hundred years. Not many schools or coaching staffs in the state can say that. Don't get me wrong. I've coached with other notable guys at other schools around this state! I've also coached with some losers too. You'll be able to pick them out soon after some interaction with them. How will you be able to tell, you ask? By whether they emulated the philosophies you are now reading.

5. *Go that extra mile.* People who are willing or truly interested in the kids' success will go that extra mile. Example, one summer, I personally spent $200 in gasoline from delivering cakes all over Alamance County as a fund-raiser for wrestling camp at Duke. It's an amount I'll never be able to recoup, so I guess I would be coaching wrestling for $200 less that year. Buying a kid on your team a hotdog. Sitting on the bus after an away game with a kid who has no money while his teammates go on to eat. Giving a kid a ride home to or from practice or after a game because he has no other way home. My old Ford F-150, the Mule, has over 900,000 miles on it, and probably 600,000 of those are giving kids a ride home. Going to events at the school on weekends that aren't academically or sports-oriented to see a player or student of yours participate in another activity in which they're involved. One time, I drove an hour to Winston-Salem on a Saturday night to see my tiny 100-pound wrestler play in a band. I drove from Graham to watch him participate in the middle of the gym in a Christmas concert at Mt. Tabor High, where I was working at the time. All week long, he'd reminded or asked me if I would show up for his performance. I knew how important it was to him

and made up my mind I couldn't miss it. So here we are, him perched in front of a big bass drum with a big drum mallet gripped in one hand. Surrounded by his fellow band members just playing away while he sat there motionless, he looked up in the crowd and found me immediately and winked with a big grin. Of course, I acknowledged, waving back. Now came the hilarious part. The band played and played and played. On around three occasions per song, the band director would point to him, and he would hit the big bass drum during the song. His part may have seemed minor, but he felt the joy of the moment if not for just a little while. Always remember that what may seem trivial or minor to us are lifetime memories for them. The impact you make on a young person's life as a teacher and coach could never be measured in this book, only by God. Going that extra mile means organizing all sorts of fund-raisers to get your team in a position where they can have the best opportunity for success. This means great self-sacrifice. By now maybe, or hopefully, you've changed your mind of what it's like to be a teacher or a coach and a successful one at that. Maybe I have recruited you, or worse yet, scared you off. You're even asking yourself, Coach, are you crazy?

6. *Make it fun, kiddo—simple.* If you aren't having fun, and even more importantly, the kids aren't having an

enjoyable time, then something is wrong. Kids will find something good in any situation, especially if they see you trying hard. Make humor, not at any student's expense, but possibly your own. They need to know you're not afraid to make a mistake or point a finger at yourself. When they know you're not afraid of being human, they feel more comfortable around you and in their own skin as well.

7. *Surrogate father.* It's very important to understand that in the old days, as well as today, you must maintain a certain distance between yourself and your students, all the while never letting them lose sight that you care about them as individuals. You must maintain your professional distance while being there with a shoulder to cry on, playing the role of a counselor. You are a giver of advice and, at the same time, discipline, tempered with love and respect. Respect, not only for those you teach, but those you work with as well, is critical. And probably, the most important, respect for your profession or craft. Scolding and praising, motivating and supporting all under the surrogate-father heading. They are all ours, so love them and always follow the rule: "How would I want my child to be treated in this situation?" If you react in this manner, you as a quality person will win out with the right decision that's best for the kids. Remember, popularity has nothing to do with

it. You're not in a popularity contest. You are in one of the most important positions on this earth. You are a teacher. An influencer of hundreds of future generations.

Now, as I said earlier, you may not agree wholeheartedly with these philosophies, and who knows, you could change or could be different altogether. Remember one thing though, no matter what the undertaking, set the rules. Go over them and don't have too many. You can rule yourself to death. But enforce the ones you have equally and with continuity, with the same consequences for everybody. Consistency is crucial.

The most notable coaches and teachers love the kids, and on good days or bad days, they never lose sight of that. These are the ones who are successful. They love their craft and are satisfied in knowing that they're making a difference in a young person's life. They certainly aren't doing it for the money. They even must spend, in most cases, the piddly amount they make on the students and on school supplies in many cases. So now you know what us old folks call, "For the love of the game." I've enjoyed my associations with many students and fellow coaches, both friends and opponents. After all, they are in the business for the same reason I am, for the kids, watching their successes and guiding them. I've also enjoyed all the travels associated with coaching, to Las Vegas, Nevada; Monmouth, New Jersey; Athens, Georgia; Ohio, and other parts of the country as well as across North Carolina. It was interesting to meet people in a faraway part of the United States who spoke differently from us but had the same basic philosophies about coaching as my colleagues and me. We just had different strategies and ideas on how to obtain and reach for goals. Not only did we share and learn, but in our sharing of ideas, they learned from us. I remember this along with all those ideas and life experiences that I've shared with so many people, such as my grandfather with all his sayings that bolstered my experience that I would need down the road. Or that wonderful grandmother who would ride my Honda 750-4 motorcycle while going down the interstate, carrying her fishing pole to her favorite spot. My life as a teacher and coach has taken me down a road unique to all others. I'm sure there are many out there who feel the same about their lives. My roller-coaster life I feel is just beginning, and yeah, I agree with you. If I hadn't lived this trail of triumphs, tragedies, miscues, and fortunes, I probably wouldn't believe it either. So I'll leave with two sentiments. Next time you see a teacher or a coach, hug them. They deserve it. And number two, I quoted myself with an adage I said at the end of the school year to every class I ever taught in all my years. "If anything I said during this semester or school year helps you in life, then it was all worthwhile. Never let anyone keep you from reaching your life goals, nothing, even those goals are subject to change. God bless you all, you will always be my students, and I'm here for you."

The End.

OTHER VOICES

Teacher, coach, comedian, and friend. These are all words that one can use to describe William Anderson "Andy" Hawks. As a matter of fact, I myself have used all of these, and a few more, to describe Coach Hawks to all my friends and family over the past ten years.

I met Andy Hawks in 1999 when I accepted a teaching job at Cummings High School. I had moved to Burlington, North Carolina, from a small town in Southeastern Ohio. Coach Hawks was one of the first people I met, and he has remained a good friend to this day.

The first thing one notices about Andy when they meet him is his "country" sense of humor. He is quick with a joke and carries it out well with his Southern accent. This quality makes him the center of attention at a social gathering. A person may not remember the gathering but will always remember Coach Hawks.

Andy Hawks is more than a coach and country comedian. He is a good teacher as well as a great friend. It seems every couple of weeks, a person will stop by the school or post a comment on Facebook looking for Coach Hawks or making a statement about how he greatly influenced their education. To me, this is the mark a great teacher has left behind and how they will influence others in the future.

As a friend, there are few better. I have seen Andy go out of his way to help those around him. Be it giving a child low on cash, a job, or taking a friend into his home. It does not matter. He will do what it takes to help a friend in need.

—Chad A. Cook

Many people come and go in our life and may influence your life in many different ways. Any person who is part of your life affects you in some kind of way. Most people would say the biggest influence on their life is their mom or dad or grandparent, but my biggest influence is Mr. Andy Hawks or Coach Hawks as some know him. Hawks is a biology and earth science teacher here at Cummings and has taught at many schools around North Carolina from Martinsville to Eastern Alamance. Coach Hawks is a man with wisdom, guidance, and a unique humor. Hawks is a man of dedication and will always bend over backward to help someone in need. The first time I met Coach Hawks was during football season when he asked me, "What do you plan to do when football season is over?" So I replied, "I don't know." He then suggested that I join the school's wrestling team. At first, I have to admit I didn't want to. I told him that I'm not sure if I can. I don't know the rules. I just gave him any excuse I could think of, but then he told me that, "You never know what you can do until you try." So after his encouraging words, I decided to join the team, and I never left after that. The first day of practice we had, he told everyone in the room that, "It doesn't matter how strong you are or how big you are. To win at this sport, it's about who wants it more and who gives the effort." Those words stuck with me throughout my four years of wrestling for Coach Hawks.

During those years, I became close to Coach Hawks and realized that he wasn't just teaching us how to wrestle but was showing us how to live life and preparing us for the world after high school. He showed me that what you put into something is what you get out of it and showed me that you have to dedicate yourself to something; there is no life in between. I've seen Hawks do countless things for students no matter what you feel about him or what you say, he is always willing to be there. I've seen him pick up kids from their houses on the bus when they didn't have a ride. I've seen him give money to kids who forgot to bring it or who just don't have it. He is always willing to sacrifice for others because he's a big-hearted person and believes in giving all that you have instead of half doing things. Hawks has shown me that sometimes, you have to do things you don't want to just because you have to. It's been times where I didn't want to come to practice, or I was hurt and didn't feel like doing things, but I did anyway because I knew in my mind he was going to be there no matter what. He taught me that sometimes you have to do what you don't want to do in order to get things done. Now that I'm graduating, I realize I wasn't going to wrestling practice for four years, I was being taught lessons of life.

Another lesson I learned from Hawks was to always give 100 percent. Whenever I missed a practice or played around in practice, he'd always say, "Give this your all because if you miss a practice or don't give it your all, who knows how good you can be." If I lost a match and missed a practice, he'd say, "Now if you wouldn't have missed that practice, you could have learned a move you didn't know or just been a little more in shape to win." He always said don't live your life in what he calls the "could had did" or the "man, if only I." He always stressed how matter how good or bad, you do give it your all, and that will not only satisfy him, but you feel good about your-self knowing you gave it all you had. Hawks stressed that life is all about your heart. With Hawks's constant dedi-cation and kindness, it made me want to do good by him and want to wrestle. If Hawks was to ever stop coaching, I would have had to quit because his motivation was the only thing that kept me on the tam. Every match that I lost during my career, I'd be upset and angry, but Hawks was always there to pick me up, and he'd always tell me, "Hey, I've won a lot in my day, I'm not upset at you, if you gave it your best that's all that matters, don't worry your time will come."

This year, I fell one match short of going to the state, and it crushed me because now I think, what if I didn't miss this practice or did that last push-up or just ran a little harder, would I have won? I believe if I would have listened to his advice more, I could have done better, but that's something I will never know. I appreciate everything Coach Andy Hawks has done for me, and if God permits, I'd like for him to one day teach my kids the same thing he has taught me. Coach Hawks is like my second father, and I can't thank him enough for helping me throughout my years of high school whether it be schoolwork or anything he's always there. To the world, you might be one person, but to one person you might be the world.

—Stacey Watlington, 5/20/07

Subj: ANDY HAWKS
Date: 5/30/2003 10:27 PM, Eastern Standard Time
From: xxxxxxxxx
To: xxxxxxx

It seems as if it was just the other day when I started going to high school and feeling so small and alone and feeling like I was absolutely a nobody. Everyone wants to feel powerful and get attention and at the same time become mentally, emotionally, physically, and morally stronger. My sophomore year in high school, I met a man named Andy Hawks. He talked me into joining the wrestling team; he was the coach. Joining the wrestling team was probably one of the greatest choices that I have ever made. By my senior year, not only did I become stronger as an athlete but Coach Hawks was also like a mentor to me. He was like a father that shouldn't let me give up on myself not only in the sport but also to become a better person. He was like a brother that kept kicking me and hitting me when he knew that I was slacking and could have done a better job. He was like a television reporter that ran around trying to get my face in front of the camera. He was a like a homeless person that held up a sign with a double meaning to make you stop and think. And later, when you walk away, the meaning makes perfect sense and changes your life because of that one sign and who it came from. Hawks was like a replacement heart that you absolutely need for surgery to live another day. He was like a weight lifting machine that always enhanced your physical being with every push. He was like the Bible, where everything is true inside; although you don't want to admit that that truth is what is actually good for you, and it will help you to become that better person and to share those morals of truth to others everywhere.

By looking at him with his red hair and blue eyes, it's hard to imagine that this one man can hold all of these traits at once. But from the help of that one man, I feel a lot bigger, a lot more powerful, and important. I have received more attention than I ever thought that I deserved. I am mentally, emotionally, physically, and morally stronger. I am that better person because of one choice and the greatest coach ever!

—David McGowan, May 29, 2003

I have known Andy for several years. I coached against his teams at Graham and Bartlett-Yancey and coached with him at Cummings. His kids always competed hard and by the rules. This is an attribute of a good coach. I have been in his classroom and observed his kids learning also, a good attribute of a good teacher.

When I came to Cummings in 1998, Andy was one of the first to welcome me and tell me he was glad I was joining the Cavalier's staff. Andy has always treated people fairly and has on more than one occasion given kids (players and classroom students) the benefit of the doubt. And a second and sometimes third chance to prove themselves. He did in in the classroom and on the playing field.

He constantly transported kids to and from school activities when they didn't have a ride, especially those early Saturday mornings of wrestling tournaments and of course at night when the tournament was over, and no one was there to pick the kids up. He also made sure kids didn't go hungry; if any of his teams stopped to eat and someone didn't have enough money for food, he would make sure they got something to eat.

Andy has a great sense of humor and is always around to lighten moments when needed, give advice and comfort when called on. He's is one of the only people I know that constantly makes me laugh in his presence. He is a good friend and fellow coach, and we have missed him this year.

I was one of the people with Andy when he was lying on the floor in his biology class that morning. It was very difficult to see a good friend and colleague struggle for life. It was an emotional few minutes for us all. It was a time if you walked into the room and didn't know anything about the person lying on the floor; you quickly became aware of how the people around him felt about him and were doing everting from giving CPR to yelling encouragement for him to "stay with us."

Thank goodness he has recovered and again is back to being the old Andy. Our kids missed him last year and this year and are always glad when they see him on the sidelines watching them compete. He's is one of their biggest supporters. We are very glad he is back coaching our wrestling team and again is a part of the coaching staff.

Andy is a unique individual, and I am proud to call him my friend.

—E. Brent Shepherd
Business education teacher/assistant football coach
Cummings High School

Andy as an athlete, student, and community leader can be characterized in two defining words, *hard work*. Hard word is all Andy knows and is his recipe for success.

Honesty is a trademark of Andy. What he says and what he does is exactly what you can expect. He never deviates from what he tells you and what he is going to do.

Attitude represents his personality. Quiet in nature and goes about his activities with a positive attitude that everyone can see and appreciate.

Respect is another attribute of Andy. Everyone who comes in contact with Andy receives his respect regardless of who you are, colleague, student, or a member of the community.

As a young man in the educational profession, you could not ask for anyone more *dedicated* than Andy. Whether it's preparing lessons, game plans, or making plans to work with students with special needs, Andy is always ready, making sure all t's are crossed and all i's dotted. The many teaching, coaching, and community awards he has received is evidence of this dedication. His *wisdom* goes far beyond his age. Knowing what to say and when to say it and making everyone feel important helps each person work harder to reach his or her potential regardless of their circumstances.

Ownership is another attribute of Andy. He buys into everything he is asked to do. He believes that he must show that he is committed in order to have others to believe and to buy into his activity whether it is a student learning a new lesson or an athlete learning a new move or play. He is proud of each activity, and his students are proud as well. This makes them successful.

With ownership comes *results*. Andy is committed to his work and has high expectations for himself, his students, and everyone else associated with his work or programs. Andy has the wisdom and knowledge to put associates in positions to be successful and attain the results he and they expect.

Kindness is beyond reproach with Andy. He has never met a stranger and treats others as he would want them to treat him. His kindness reaches all areas of the school and community that he lives in. We are taught that we should love others as we love ourselves. Andy's kindness truly represents this love.

Andy is a very special young man. He truly represents all the HARD WORK that we expect from a member of our teaching family.

—Bill Joye
Football Coach
Graham High School
NCHSAA
March 19, 2001

Andy Hawks
Cummings High School
2200 North Mebane Street
Burlington NC 27217

Dear Andy,

We are doing a "Wall of Champions," which would be a high school sports history of our best coaches, athletes, officials, and booking agents.

Through this letter, we are asking you to send us either a 5×7 or 8×10 photo of yourself. We would also ask you to write ay comments you would like on your picture. Please sign ***To the NCHSAA***, include your comments, and sign your name. As soon as we receive your picture, we will have it matted, framed, and then we will hang it on our "Wall of Champions."

We look forward to hearing from you as soon as possible, but no later than April 2001, if you are willing to participate in this project so that we can plan on our wall space.

In closing, let us thank you for your cooperation in this matter. We are very proud of you and would like to honor you as one of our best.

Sincerely,
Charlie Adams
Executive Director

CA/phl

Cc: Martha Land, President, NCHSAA
Charles Long, Vice-President, NCHSAA

"In the Huddle"   Times News Varsity.com

Get Well, Andy
October 11, 2007 by sschramm

Wrestling is a different kind of sport. It asks so much of its competitors yet gives such humble return. To be good, a kid must put in hours upon hours of practice to make themselves strong but lithe, explosive but relentless. And if they don't make weight, it can be all for naught. It's also a sport that exists in a level of obscurity. College scholarships are scarce. Its biggest start are far from household names and the most decorated high school standouts, rarely ever Big Man on Campus status. There's something about slipping into one of those revealing singlets that strips most people of all pretense. Bottom line, everyone who competes is there for the love of the sport and little else. Maybe that's why it can be pretty fun to cover. The kids, coaches, and fans are real. They love their sport and respect everyone who practices it. This sense of community makes wrestling tournaments feel less like competitions and more like social gatherings with headgear, funny shoes, and the occasional blood timeout. Cummings coach Andy Hawks is a fixture in this world. He is one of several talented area wrestling coaches that I've had the privilege to work with and learn about the sport from. With his bright red hair and a mischievous glint in his eye, Hawks kept you laughing and made you feel like you were always in on the joke. In my years on the beat, I've seen Hawks comfort his kids after crushing losses and rush to their aid after an injury. Heck, one Thanksgiving he had a few kids stay with him while their parents left town. They wanted to wrestle in a tournament, so Hawks made room for them in his home and at his table. One thing was always clear with Hawks, if you competed for him, he had your back. Always. Maybe that was why when he collapsed in class on Wednesday morning, his students rushed to get help, help that proved to be lifesaving. They had his back too. Right now, Hawks is in a Durham hospital, and the Cummings community is hoping for the best.

I'm sure those in wrestling, a sport whose heart is in the right place, are doing the same.

Andy Hawks can be the most unassuming kid's mentor and motivate them to perform at very high levels on and off the field. He mixes life's lessons with his unique down-home humor that puts everyday problems into perspective. Andy has, in his own life, overcome many obstacles to reach his own goals. His personal life experiences give him a unique insight into the world of his students, as well as the problems they face in everyday life.

—Jay Perdue
Athletic Director
Cummings High School
Burlington, NC

About the Author

Andy Hawks, born November 2, 1954, on a farm in Graham, North Carolina, on the banks of Haw River, was raised by his grandparents Oscar and Tacey Hawks. Here he learned the meaning and habit of hard work, strong values, and social skills that would serve him throughout life.

His love for athletics made him an accomplished athlete in high school. Being coached by many different and successful coaches, he decided to attempt to do for many others what had been done for him.

Helping to shape lives and teaching others how to make decisions that will help them throughout is the most satisfying feeling anyone could have.

In following these endeavors, he has been fortunate enough to receive the following awards:

Member of NCHSAA Wall of Fame

Member of Hugh M. Cummings Athletic Hall of Fame 2014

Most-winning wrestling coach in Hugh M. Cummings High School history

Twenty times Wrestling Coach of the Year

Led Cummings High School to eighteen conference wrestling championships

Inducted multiple times to the Who's Who of American Teachers

Dickies Work Apparel American Worker of the Year in the US 1997

Coached eighteen conference championships in football

As an assistant football coach, he also helped lead Cummings High School to the 2002 and 2006 state football championships.

He also coached state runners-up in football in 2001 and 2003.